the Rusty Nail

Issue 14, April 2013

Editor-in-Chief
Craig A. Hart

Cover Design
Paul Brand

Published by Sweatshoppe Publications

The Rusty Nail

CONTENTS

In the Great Pharmaceutical Warehouse
by Jim Meirose, Page 3
Burying the Clocks
by Catherine Zickgraf, Page 6
Violining
by Catherine Zickgraf, Page 6
Those Golden Curls
by Allen Coin, Page 7
Paisley
by Catherine Zickgraf, Page 9
Lightning's Final Dash
by James Curtiss, Page 10
Freeing Me
by Benjamin Grossman, Page 13
Winter's Cinema
by Roman Colombo, Page 14
Habemus Papam
by Kenneth Hickey, Page 15
Snarling Metal
by Michael Plesset, Page 15
Glimmer
by Patrick Jackson, Page 16
A Tiger By the Tale
by Gary Clifton, Page 18
Closer Than the Other Side of the World
by David Seguin, Page 19
Masochism
by e.a.d.sellors, Page 22
Anarchy in the U.S.
by Paul Reilly, Page 23
Medicine
by e.a.d. sellors, Page 25
The Sycamore Tree
by Niall O'Connor, Page 26
Reunion
by Gary Clifton, Page 28
Loneliness
by Patrick Jamieson, Page 29
Thoroughly Modern
by Kirsten Mullen, Page 30
Moving Out After the Divorce
by Stephanie Bradbury, Page 30
Two-Ton Paperweight
by Pat Malone, Page 31
Stop Holding On
by M.N. O'Brien, Page 33
Of Higgs and Flame
by Matthew Sissom, Page 34
Protest
by Annemarie Ni Churreain, Page 36
Thermonuclear Daydreams
by Douglas Sterling, Page 37

Out of the Closet
by Michael Price, Page 38
The Accidental Florist
by Marian Brooks, Page 39
Toxic
by Lindsey Appleton, Page 39
Fiction
by e.a.d. sellors, Page 39
6 More Drinks
by Neil Randall, Page 40
Menace of the Rainbow
by Meg Tuite, Page 40
A Cracker Ambush
by Bob Kalkreuter, Page 41
Elements
by Kimberly Zook, Page 44
Skylark
by February Grace, Page 45
Poet
by February Grace, Page 45
Speechless
by February Grace, Page 45
Movie Star
by Alan Haider, Page 45
D.B.
by Kathryn Lynch, Page 46
Biker Queen Fishing Story
by Timmy Reed, Page 47
Between Princess and Power Queens
by Kate O'Reilley, Page 49
Fall's Fossils
by Diane Webster, Page 50
Rain Thaw
by Diane Webster, Page 50
Between the Lines
by Diane Webster, Page 50

The Rusty Nail Staff

Editor-in-Chief
Craig A. Hart

Associate Editor
Dr. Kimberly Nylen Hart

Graphic Design Editor
Paul Brand

www.rustynailmag.com
rustynailmag@gmail.com
@rustynailmag

In the Great Pharmaceutical Warehouse

by Jim Meirose

In the great pharmaceutical warehouse, Sebastian, Bobby, and Jolly worked on the order packing line packing drugs into boxes and pushing them off onto the line to the loading docks. They worked at a steel table being fed orders from the picking line on a conveyor and the bright green trays full of yellow boxes and bottles and tubes came to them; quickly, they formed cardboard boxes they took from the palletloads of folded boxes behind them and threw the green trays of pharmaceuticals into the boxes, sealed the boxes with heavy tape, staplehammered the order sheets onto the boxes, and pushed the boxes off onto the line to the docks. Jolly, a small older black man, worked alone at a packing table and Sebastian and Bobby worked at another, facing each other from opposite sides of the table, with the line of orders separating them. All day, they talked as they packed; the topics varied; this day, it was Sebastian's favorite; unionizing. Their hands moved fast doing the work as they spoke to each other even faster.

I tell you Bobby—we need a union here. We don't make shit.

Well—what do you expect to make in a shit job like this?

We could do better—hey Jolly—Jolly!

Jolly turned around at his packing table and said What Sebastian?

Jolly, says Sebastian—don't you think we should be unionized?

Jolly shook his staplehammer as he spoke.

I told you, I agree with you. We'd do better unionized. But no one will stand up and do the work required to make it happen—everybody's afraid for their jobs. That bastard Massingill will fire anybody who even whispers the word union.

Bobby turned and faced Jolly.

Why don't you stand up Jolly? Are you afraid—

Damn straight I'm afraid—jobs are hard to find out there.

Bobby turned back to Sebastian.

What about you, he said. You talk big—why don't you stand up?

I—

All at once an announcement came over the public address system.

Sebastian to the office please—Sebastian Sodoma—to the office please—

Well, said Bobby—what's this all about?

Damned if I know, said Sebastian, putting down his staplehammer. He made his way around stacks of boxes and headed for the door to the office at the front of the warehouse.

Mr. Massingill wants to see you, said a secretary. Go right in.

Sebastian entered Massingill's office. The tall blonde man sat behind his high gloss desk and motioned for Sebastian to take a seat and said Close the door, Sebastian.

Sebastian sat and Massingill leaned forward and tapped a finger on the desk.

Sebastian, I'll get right to the point. How would you like to be in management?

What? said Sebastian—why me—management?

Right. You're young, you've got the drive—we've been watching you Sebastian. The other men look up to you. How about it? I don't believe in wasting time—you'll be co-foreman with Panko back in the warehouse. It's too big for him to handle alone. Well?

Well what—

Well, said Massingill, half rising—will you take the job or not?

Yes. I will.

Good—now you just sit here a minute while I go out and get hold of Panko.

Massingill quickly left the office. There had been a single sheet of paper on the desk before him. Sebastian couldn't resist looking at it. He rose and went over.

The paper held two columns. The heading above the first said FOR PROMOTION; and his own name was below it. The heading above the second said FOR LAYOFF; and when he saw there were two names under it, he quickly went back to his chair and sat down for fear of having been discovered finding out such a secret.

Bobby and Jolly's names were in that column—FOR LAYOFF—Sebastian thought the first thing he needed to do when he got out on the floor was to tell Bobby and Jolly about it—but then he thought—I am management now, I can't tell them, but, they need to know—his stomach churned as he sat there staring at the paper atop the desk.

Massingill came back in with fat Panko, the senior warehouse foreman, who wore his usual tight short sleeved white shirt and short wide tie.

This is your partner now Panko, said Massingill—take him back and show him the ropes.

Okay, said Panko—congratulations Sebastian. Welcome aboard.

Sebastian rose and shook both men's hands but his thoughts were with Bobby and Jolly.

Panko led Sebastian back into the warehouse and they went to Panko's glassed-in office and Panko said well I guess that's your desk there—I wondered why they moved a second desk into this office—but now I know.

Panko—there's something I need to—to talk to you about.

What?

There was a sheet of paper in Massingill's office that said Bobby and Jolly are up to be laid off.

What? You looked at a paper on Massingill's desk?

I couldn't help it—

Panko rubbed his chin and looked through the window out toward the packing line.

I'm stunned, said Panko. Bobby and Jolly are two of my best men—

And they've both got years with the company, Panko—now here we go. If there was a union their jobs would be safe.

Safe? Why?

Because they've got a lot of seniority—and they've both got families to feed—I'll tell you what Panko—I don't care that he just made me management—I think Bobby and Jolly should be told. Maybe they can start organizing—maybe they can get a union in here—

Don't talk that way, said Panko sternly. Massingill knew you just said that, he'd fire you.

What do you believe Panko?

What do you mean what do I believe?

Do you think it would be right to get rid of Bobby and Jolly?

He bored his fierce look into Panko's face. The heavier man looked away.

I'll decide what they know and what they don't know, said Panko. They're in my area of the warehouse—it's me who'll suffer if they get let go. I'll have to shuffle men around and try and get two in there who can pack like they can.

Then there's no reason you should have to suffer Panko. Please—try and save them.

Save them?

Their jobs. Save their jobs any way that you can.

Panko stared at Sebastian a minute then spoke harshly.

We never had this conversation Sebastian—you understand that? And you never looked at that paper on Massingill's desk either. And you're going to say nothing to Bobby and Jolly. Now let's go back to the shipping docks and the returns and the bulk storage area. That's what you'll be in charge of and that's all you should have on your mind. Understood?

Listen Panko—I think—

Don't think! You're management now, but you're junior to me. I could get you fired. So shape up, you understand. Don't butt into my area.

Okay.

They spent the rest of the day looking over the areas of the warehouse that were now Sebastian's to manage. Sebastian did not return to his packing station and saw little of Bobby and Jolly for the next several days. He stayed back in the areas he was responsible for but thought he noticed that Panko was spending a lot more time around the packing area than he had when Sebastian had been a packer. Over the next few weeks he noticed from afar that Bobby and Jolly were leaving the packing station for about an hour each day and were going around talking to other workers up the line—the checkers, the pickers, the stockers. But he never went up front to see what was going on. But the day finally came when Panko and he were in the glass house together doing paperwork and it suddenly struck him to speak.

Panko.

What?

What's going on with Bobby and Jolly.

What do you mean what's going on?

I notice they spend a lot of time talking to the other workers all around your area of the warehouse—they spend a lot of time off the packing line. Why is that?

Panko sat back and spread a hand out on his paperwork.

You know what Sebastian?

No. What?

It's really none of your God-damned business.

Oh—okay. I'll stop wondering about it then.

Sebastian thought it best to toe the line around Panko, since he was the junior foreman and Panko could make things touch for him if he got out of line.

A few more days passed and then there came an announcement over the public address system.

Panko, Bobby, Jim Jolly—come to the office—Panko, Bobby, Jim Jolly—

Then, after that announcement and for hours after that, Panko, Bobby, and Jolly were gone. Sebastian had the glass walled office to himself—then came another announcement.

Sebastian—come to the office—Sebastian—

Sebastian found himself standing in front of Massingill's large dark wooden desk.

Sebastian, I'm promoting you, said Massingill—you've got the whole warehouse now.

Me? Why? What about Panko?

I let Panko go.

What?

Yes—let him go—and Bobby and Jolly too.

What? Wow—why?

They were working to organize a union back there in the warehouse, Sebastian. Panko was letting them do union organizing on company time. Do you know anything about that Sebastian? Do you know anything about this union stuff and what's been going on back in the warehouse?

I—I feel the men back there should be unionized. I won't lie.

What? You do?

Yes. I talked to Panko about it. I talked to Bobby and Jolly about it too.

So it was you who put them up to it?

I won't lie about something I believe in. I suppose I put them up to it.

Have you been trying to organize the men in your area of the warehouse?

No. But I should—

Well you'll have no such chance. You're fired too. Get the hell off my property.

Because I believe in something enough that I won't lie about it you're firing me? For being that kind of man?

No. You're fired for stirring up trouble in my warehouse. Get the hell off the property now, Sebastian—you're a no good sneaky little lying twirp.

I never lied—

You're lying right now. Get out of my sight.

You'll be sorry someday Mr. Massingill. You'll be sorry for how you hurt people—

Get out!

Now!

Sebastian left. As he left the building, Massingill called Irene Rome into his office. Irene was an up-and-comer; it was time and the need was now there to promote her.

Irene stood before Massingill's desk.

What can I do for you, Mr. Massingill?

Irene—you ever thought of being promoted?

Promoted? Yes, I've been hoping for it, but—

Well then as of now you're the warehouse foreman. I've let the other foremen go.

Who was that?

Never mind—it's not important.

I don't know a thing about how the warehouse works, Mr. Massingill.

You watch the men and make sure they all keep moving, said Massingill—you watch the flow of the orders from the office to the loading docks. Let's go for a walk out back there, I'll show you how the place runs. It's not complicated. You just need to keep everything moving.

They went out to the warehouse and Massingill showed her the flow of the place. They walked along the line until they got to the packing stations, where Sebastian Bobby and Jolly used to work. Joel Singlet, a small man who was normally a checker, was the lone packer on duty. The lines were very backed up.

This is an area that needs attention, Massingill told Irene. We've got to get some help in here—we lost the three packers we had and we need to hire here. Maybe hire some contractors who have warehouse experience. Contractors are cheaper then regular employees. That's something I expect you to take care of. You're familiar with the process of how we hire contractors—I know that. Isn't that right?

Yes, said Irene.

In the days and weeks that followed Irene managed the warehouse and realized it all pretty much ran itself—the men were experienced and knew what to do. She put an ad in the paper for contractors too put on the packing line. Checking was suffering for lack of Joel Singlet and she needed to act quickly. She interviewed several men who answered the ad and finally hired on who stood out; who had worked in a pharmaceutical warehouse before; who had actually done a packing job. She hired him on without telling Massingill because he had told her he expected her to handle it—and she wanted to take full responsibility. Being promoted was a big opportunity for Irene. She put Joel Singlet back on checking and brought in a second contractor and paid special attention to the packing area and before long, it was humming. She felt proud that Massingill seldom came out into the warehouse to check on her and never called her up to his office to see what she might need—he trusted her to run the place herself without help—she was especially proud of having handled bringing in the contractors and getting the pasking area up to snuff. She was dismayed, however, that after the contractors were on the job a week, Massingill laid off two men from the loading dock area without consulting her. She guessed he thought that since she had brought in two people to do packing, he could let go two people from another area. Irene spoke to the contractor doing the packing and complained to him that she was down two men in the back because of Massingill; she had grown to like the man and was impressed with his work, and especially was impressed that he was a good listener. She often confided in him since he was not a real employee, she thought it an innocent thing to do. After the layoffs she was in the packing area and chatted with the contractor.

The big boss up front is making my life hard, she said.

His hands moved quickly packing as he answered her.

Why is that?

He's let two men go from the dock without even asking me about it. He's told me he's going to replace everybody with contractors over time. Says these jobs just need strong backs and weak minds. Why should the company invest in employees for this kind of work?

Is that what he says?

Yes. Between you and me, I'm not sure how much I like him.

The man nodded agreement as he pushed the next box off onto the line.

She went back to her office to do paperwork and the packer worked quickly to burn off his anger at what she had told him. He knew what she was talking about; he'd seen people laid off before—he'd been laid off himself. And he knew how tough the warehouse foreman job was and how Irene must feel. He kept his opinions to himself, though, until one day Massingill unexpectedly appeared walking past the packing stations to take care of some things that twere happening in the back. The contractor laid down his staplehammer and approached Massingill. He pointed sharply at the tall blonde manager and shouted.

You, he said—you've got no feelings for the people who work so hard back here—I',m told you let more people go and plan to let the whole place go over time—you bastard! These people have families to feed and mortgages to pay—

Sebastian! Exclaimed Massingill—Sebastian, what are you doing back in my warehouse?

Irene hired me on, said Sebastian—you are a bastard Massingill—a rotten stinking unfeeling coldhearted bastard—

Massingill stood there trembling with anger. He pointed at Sebastian.

Okay—get out of the building! Your time here is over! Once and for all! And yes I will let everybody go—just to spite you, you little twirp—noww I'm going to make sure I end up letting everybody go!

You Bastard!

Get out!

Having heard the shouting, Irene rushed up from the loading dock.

What's going on here—Mr. Massingill—what's the problem—Ronnie! What's wrong, why are you yelling at Mr. Massingill—

Ronnie, said Massingill—he told you his name is Ronnie—no! This is Sebastian! I fired him once already and now I'm firing him again—and you, too, Irene, for having been stupid enough to not check with me before you brought in any contractors.

Oh! snapped Sebastian. You're going to fire Irene too—

Damn straight I am! And there's not a damned thing you can do about it. Now—I told you twice already—get the hell off my property—both of you!

Having been fired twice now, Sebastian left, as did Irene. He asked her to dinner as they walked to their cars and she accepted—they could cry in their beer together now. Ultimately, the two were married—but that is a whole other story. They really ended up in heaven. Massingill stewed in his own juices over time; ultimately, he was let go too, and finally lost his mind. Now he wanders the streets bellowing orders into the air; but there is no one listening any more.

• • •

Burying the Clocks
by Catherine Zickgraf

Stark of stars, the ceiling swelled when we gathered
where she lay, pink-suited, asleep,
whom we'd elevate to the vinyl eaves.
Then we headed south with tears in our mouths.

Mom gave Grandmom a baby girl
to grow in her lap and nap in her gowns.
We'd walk to town by the railroad tracks
where ghost trains still whistle out back.

Last year, as she plattered up deer for her family,
I dragged spare chairs from the webs of spare rooms.
Her sons and their sons centered the table,
those hunters teething at bones wet with meat.

She stored dimes for the times a son mowed her hill,
his own stubborn heart repeating with hers.
Where are her knotted telephone lines?
I need her to nuzzle the children I'll birth.

Asking admits I don't know the answer.
Even in dreams every clock has its place—
all laid one by one where the roots of her oak
suspend them in the space of her ocean of earth.

• • •

Catherine Zickgraf *is a writer first, a performer second. As Catherine the Great, she has shared her spoken word from Boston to Miami to San Francisco and scores of stages in between. See her perform at youtube.com/czickgraf*

Yet the written word is her first love. Her writing has appeared in the Journal of the American Medical Association, Pank, Bartleby-Snopes, and GUD Magazine.

Violining
by Catherine Zickgraf

This pale afternoon,
I climb the brick back stairs of the
Carmen de la Victoria house for
esteemed university guests.
The empty corridor echoes
up tall walls, through the board floor.
The visiting violinist has invited me
to the conservatory in his temporary domicile.

The lower levels fall quiet each after-lunch siesta,
while daily he labors in a lofty corner
of the Andalusian mansion.
His violin lures toward his quarters,
I twist around stairs in their cases.
A mahogany door stops the steps
at the peak of *Carmen*'s tiled spire.

I hear his wand furiously stir his ceiling atmosphere,
forcing song toward me through the iron keyhole.
Perhaps his abode holds a broad forest of attackers,
at whom he flings notes in skillful directions.
Or maybe he stands steering his bed
through a storm of white noise.
In there, leaning into his bow, he could be
soothing the boiling waves of floor-flooding silence.

Under his door slide sheets of fire.
I shrink into the old molding,
clamping my head—
I'm powerless to its throbbing.
Bending graphs and curving nets
spiral behind my eyes,
so I steady myself against the thick window.

I yearn for an art, a talent,
the desire to work at something.
I'll wander uninspired, blocked for a decade.
While exploding in his room,
the Ancients once traveling the Spanish paths
inspire him into discipline.
May they immortalize him one day
into stone.

Those Golden Curls
by Allen Coin

A middle-aged woman sits in her beat-up old sedan in the parking lot of Oleander Acres retirement home. Her back hunched, forehead almost touching the steering wheel, she digs through the plain brown purse sitting on her lap. She pushes aside a pocket book, small packs of tissue paper and tampons to get to the bottom of the purse. Amongst the loose change, mints, and other small items that find their way to the bottom of purses she finds her lip balm. She adjusts her rear-view mirror and briefly studies her face before liberally coating her lips with the balm. Looking at herself in the mirror and frowning, she tugs at her straight brown hair and scrunches her nose like she smells something rancid. She wraps a red lanyard around her neck, an ID card dangling from it with her name, Sandra Pickett, and picture along with her title, registered nurse, and the name of a hospital. Taped to the dashboard is a yellowed photograph which she touches lightly and sighs. She clutches her purse and climbs out of the car, adjusts her white scrubs, and marches for the automatic door of the facility with a look of determination on her face.

Inside, the woman behind the front counter smiles at Sandra and says,

"Back so soon! Do you ever get any time off?"

Sandra gives the woman a polite laugh and says, "Just lunch time. But today I had a salad from McDonald's, so, no."

The woman behind the counter gives her own obligatory polite laugh as Sandra resumes her determined march and disappears around a corner.

Ugly floral wallpaper and linoleum tiles with shades of green and blue decorate the harshly-lit hallway of the assisted living wing of Oleander Acres. Figures in scrubs pop in and out of rooms, delivering pills and taking away soiled laundry. A resident sits ancient and decrepit in her wheelchair in the middle of the hall. She covers her right eye with her right hand and announces "I can see him!" The nurses pay no attention to her. A redheaded woman and her daughter quietly emerge from a room down the hall; the woman is crying softly, the daughter's eyes wide with shock and confusion. She's too young to be here. The woman in the wheelchair observes them with her one uncovered eye as they draw nearer to her. The daughter sheepishly smiles at her as they pass and the old woman whispers, "Uh-oh."

A wide door opens nearby. Sandra pushes an old man with a long white beard and jiggling beer gut out into the hall. Hunched over the chair like an ox hauling a full load, her white scrubs crumple on her lower back in an unflattering way. As they pass the woman with her hand over her eye she says to them, "Give me your hams. Can I see your hams?" The bearded man smiles at her, and Sandra pays no attention.

A thought seems to occur to the man in the wheelchair as they roll down the hall,

"I ever tell you 'bout how I got my name, Miss—?" he says, turning his ear towards her.

"Sandra." she says. He nods as if he just needed the reminder. "Tell me the story again, Daddy Bill."

"Again?" he says, smiling. "If I must." He takes a long breath, "You see, it was nine-teen-fiddy and my young, stupid, teenage self had just bought me a motorcycle. It was a fordee-four Harley, like the ones they had in the war, except mine had a Knucklehead engine in it," he chuckles, "Mama nearly had a heart attack when she saw me on that thing... Wasn't long 'til I was ridin' with the local bike group. We weren't no *gang* like the boys out there these days, makin' trouble and doin' *drugs* and all that mess. We were civilized; about the wildest thing we ever did was go to the drive-in and talk to girls... Fact, that's how I met my wife, Doreen. She was a sight to *behold*. She had those golden curls—like Shirley Temple's, except hers were real—and it wasn't long until we were gettin' hitched 'cause she was gonna have our first baby... Boys in the group learned I was gonna be a pop and one day one of 'em called me Daddy Bill. Ever since then, everybody called me Daddy Bill, even if they weren't family."

"That's a lovely story."

"Thank ya, Miss—?"

"... Sandra."

He nods his head. "Where we goin', Miss?"

"It's dinner time, Daddy Bill. Pork chop night tonight."

"Ah, wonderful. I do love me some pork chops. Been *ages* since I had 'em, though."

The Assisted Living wing intersects the main hall of Oleander Acres. At the intersection is the TV area where cleaned-up residents are set up in their wheelchairs to await scheduled visits from children and grandchildren. Two middle-aged women with similar features—sisters—enter the TV area as a young man in his 20's—the son of one of the sisters—hangs back just far enough to not be noticed by the residents. The sisters kneel in front of a slumped over gray-haired woman in a wheelchair. She slowly picks her head up and studies the people kneeling in front of her; her facial muscles contract and quiver as she lets out a long, screaming wail. Her cry sounds more like an angry infant's than a happy adult's. The sisters motion with their hands for the young man to join them. He rubs his face and takes in a deep breath as if he's preparing to dive. When he enters her line of sight, the woman lets out another anguished cry. Between sobs and wails she says, "I'm... so... happy... to see you!"

A dry erase board on an easel next to the propped-open doors of the cafeteria reads TUESDAY NIGHT IS PORKCHOP NIGHT! They round the corner and a tall man preparing plates of food behind a sneeze guard perks up as he sees Daddy Bill coming.

"Daddy Bill! How you doin', old timer?"

"Better than that road-kill you're scoopin' I suppose. How're you, Mister—?"

The man's smile falters. "...Wayne. I'm Wayne." He looks at Sandra and she gives him a sympathetic frown. He asks Daddy Bill what he wants to eat.

"What's on the menu?" Daddy Bill says.

"Pork chops, and the usual fixin's: cornbread, green beans, mash' potatoes."

"That sounds good. I'll have all that."

"I'll have a salad." Sandra says. Her voice startles Daddy Bill, who shifts in his chair to look behind him. He opens his mouth to say something but is interrupted by Wayne,

"Here," he says, pushing a green cafeteria tray under the sneeze guard, "put this on yer lap."

Daddy Bill carefully rests the tray of food on his gut. A look of thought comes over his face, "I've heard that one before!" Wayne chuckles and Daddy Bill looks at him like a child pleased with having made his father laugh.

"Say, Wayne, why cain't an elephant ride a bicycle?"

"I dunno Daddy Bill, why *cain't* he?"

"Cause he don't got a thumb to ring the bell!"

Wayne laughs, "Have a good night, funny man." He smiles at Sandra. She halfway smiles back.

Sandra pushes Daddy Bill into the sitting area and finds a booth away from the windows. The one she chooses has a framed poster of Frank Sinatra hanging on the wall above it. She places Daddy Bill at the end of the table and locks his wheels in place as he sets the tray on the table. Taking her plate from the tray, she sits down in the booth. Daddy Bill is staring at his plate with a deep frown. He looks worried, ready to cry. He shifts his weight to look behind him over his right shoulder, then his left. He looks at the ceiling, and back at his food, and at his wheelchair. He checks his wrist, but isn't wearing a watch. He rubs his thighs, grabs the arm rests, and begins to push himself up, then notices Sandra sitting beside him holding a pepper shaker above her salad. She shoots raised eyebrows at him. His frown seems to lighten; he lets himself sink back into the wheelchair.

"You need anything, Daddy Bill?"

"Uh, no. No, I'm fine."

"Will you eat your food for me?"

"Okay," he says, picking up a piece of cornbread, pinching it into smaller pieces, "okay."

He pushes a piece of cornbread under his lip with two fingers like chewing tobacco.

"I ever tell you about my—" he says staring at the table, chewing. Sandra, leaning over her plate with a fork in her mouth, looks up at him. Daddy Bill swallows, shoves another piece of cornbread in his cheek, and continues staring for a moment, "I ever tell you 'bout how I got my name?"

"Tell me again, Daddy Bill."

They near the woman with her right eye covered. She reaches out and grabs Daddy Bill's hand. Sandra yanks the wheelchair to a halt, the momentum nearly pulling her down.

"Let me see your hams!"

Hesitating for a moment, Daddy Bill reaches out with his hands and she grabs hungrily at them. The grey-haired lady inspects his knuckles and then turns them over to rub his palms, "They're sticky!" she says with a satisfied grin on her face. She lets go and covers her eye. She points down the hallway at nobody in particular, "Here comes trouble!"

Sandra takes the opportunity to wheel Daddy Bill into his room and quickly shuts the door behind them.

"I ever tell you 'bout my daughter?" he says as he stares into the space outside his window.

"The one who's never here?"

He twists to look behind him, "Hm?"

Without a response, she turns her attention to the closet.

"My daughter, Charlotte, is the prettiest girl you'd ever know," he says while Sandra rummages through the closet, bottles of pills and vitamins rattling, "She got those golden curls, just like her mama's. She's smart, too. Graduated top of her class, you know. She's the one who gave the last speech at the ceremony. I forget what you call it." He pauses to mumble some words to himself, trying to find the right one. Sandra squints at a particular bottle, trying to read the tiny print on the label. "Anyway, she gave the *best* speech. Girls in the audience were wipin' tears from their eyes, some boys were too, I bet. Prob'ly pretending they had somethin' in their eye. She got a standing ovation. When everybody sat down I remember sayin' to my little girl sittin' next to me—" Sandra drops a bottle and the cap pops off, sending pills scattering across the floor.

"Shit," she says, getting on her knees to collect the pills. She rubs them on her shirt one-by-one and dropping them in the bottle.

"What was that last part, Daddy Bill?"

"Hm?"

"Nevermind." She sighs.

Later, Sandra helps Daddy Bill into his bed. As she folds up his wheelchair and sets it in the corner, he fumbles around with the remote and flips through a few channels. She fills a cup with tap water from the bathroom sink and sits down in the recliner next to the nightstand beside his bed. He stops on a channel—a plastic puck is bouncing down a series of metal pegs.

"Plinko," he mumbles, "Price is Right. That'll do." He sets the remote on the nightstand and folds his arms over his chest. Sandra counts out a few pills in her hand.

"Here," she hands the glass of water to Daddy Bill—he takes it obediently, "take these." She drops some pills into his big hand. He eyes them cautiously, and then downs them along with one big gulp of water. He sets the glass on the nightstand and they both relax to watch the show, hands resting on their stomachs.

The episode ends and a new one starts; people come on down from the audience to guess the prices of things. Daddy Bill is starting to doze off, and so is Sandra.

"I ever tell you…" he says. Sandra perks up and looks at him in some sort of anticipation. "bout my… daughter…" His head falls back on his pillow and within moments, he is snoring.

Quietly, she grabs the purse sitting at her feet and heads out the door, letting it softly click behind her. The hall is almost silent except for a couple of nurses chatting at the nurses' station. Most residents are in their rooms with the doors closed, falling asleep after dinner. Sandra notices one door open and looks in as she passes; the grey-haired lady is staring at the news on a TV, saying "Who's that? Who's that?"

The nurses break their conversation as Sandra approaches. They smile and one says, "Have a good night!" Sandra meekly smiles back at them without saying a word and continues on. A different woman is at the front counter. She doesn't look up from the computer and Sandra doesn't try to get her attention. The automatic doors open up and at the same time, a distant pop of thunder. It's drizzling lightly. Sandra looks up at the sky as if she is surprised to have not noticed the change in weather. She gets her keys out of her purse and jogs, not much faster than a swift walk, to her car.

In her car she wipes the rain off of her face and takes a moment to breathe and listen to the drops plinking against the sunroof. She looks over at the yellowed photograph taped to the dashboard and reaches out to grab a corner of it. She carefully pries it free and holds it close to her face.

She lets out a sigh as she studies the picture of herself as a young child with her portly ex-biker father posing and her much older valedictorian sister, dressed in cap and gown. The tassel hangs off of Charlotte's mortarboard and rests on her shoulder, frayed strands mixing with her long blond hair—those golden curls.

...

Paisley
by Catherine Zickgraf

Back in college, Nikie gifted me her treasure:
her paisley polyester blouse
patterned with red-green figures like figs.

Some nights, headed home from the library,
I'd weave my arms through its sleeves,
leaving behind books to tour the trees,
lime green in the lights
lining paths around Lake Osceola.
Ageless angels smoothed the way
as I wandered the cornerless nursery.

That shirt was magic. Complex lines and lives
snaked together geometric necks,
twisted slithering vines around each other.
I tried to follow the map they made,
searching for the end of forever.

I wore it warming up in ballet.
Then traveling home across violin fields,
I'd *tendu* pointed toes through notes like doorways.
I'd *pique* between clefs, end my dance in *releve*
though those strings to this day still play in the grass.

And some nights, Nikie and I
would climb pebble roofs to look down on our lives.
The clouds blanketing the sky sprayed rain
warm on my hair as the summer sun,
dripping drops from the tip of each strand.

Most nights, though, I set off alone.
And as wind off the lake turned
spokes of windmills unwinding in the dark,
I'd *pirouette* in pinwheels of polyester arms—
feeling my adulthood beginning,
I was newly freed to choose my own direction.

So I made my own decisions.
Though sometimes, petals hung from stems like tears,
like wombs meant to protect conception,
like eggs drooping into the earth
under shrouds of parachutes.

An amber crescent reclines beside the moon tonight.
These fifteen years later, I finally own the words to describe
my fingers of feathers surfing waves of endless sky.

Living rivers once flowing Eden
still feed the veins that branch from my heart.
My time in college is now water under a footbridge,
where manatees like ghost submarines
steer the Miami campus canals.
My home is Georgia now
where these sea cows swim invisibly
my backyard creek under nested parliaments of owls.

For four years I grew
until billows of grass at the edge of the wild
tried to untame my garden.
Now I have three boys who bring me chaos and joy.
And cornucopias in the clouds
sound harvest horns of plenty now.
While pinecones are still maturing on the boughs,
my words curve around a thousand bells,
from their golden mouths vibrations toll.

I tie yarn among long pines for my exploring children
so they too can wander their own unknown.
I watch them from the porch with gratitude
they're still young enough that they still return home.

I lost that shirt one day.
Then I graduated college for full-blown adulthood.
But adventures still fill my mind,
dreams will never leave me,
will never be fully explored—
even when my soul one day outruns my body.

Lightning's Final Dash
by James Curtiss

There was a time when no one could catch him. Beset by hands, he had feinted and spun while they'd vainly groped to halt his powerful progress. Because their pursuit was doomed to failure: in breathless despair, they were left in his wake as he passed them by with a burst of lightning speed.

And so that's why they called him 'Lightning'. But his real name was Rodney Lewis; and while she'd fretted, his mother took issue with the moniker that the papers had applied to her child. Afraid for his life, she had refused to say the name that was known through Detroit and for a moment the rest of the nation.

But the name was fine in itself though. In fact, she had burned with pride when she read it in the *News* and rather despised how he'd earned it. Because football filled her with horror: almost every night, she had dreamt that Rodney lay as dead on the field as her husband was from cancer.

Yet in high school he'd rarely been tackled. Because he was an all-American tailback; and while he played, he had shattered records as he galloped his way through defenders who'd blanched at his mention. A juking juggernaut, he was like a cyclone that tore down the field while attired in pads and cleats.

And he had reduced Ohio to terror. Yet luckily for them, there had finally come an autumn day when their prayers to the Lord were granted.

But at first he was a dreamy child. Because he'd been born in the 1940s; and as he grew up, the fact that he was black had affected his life as he lived in the Motor City. A powder-keg, race relations throughout Detroit were as polluted as its offal-filled rivers.

And eventually that keg exploded. It was building up, and in '67 there was a riot so fierce that it had required National Guardsmen. But that day was still in the future: as he dreamed away, Rodney thought less about things like race than he did about his burning obsession.

Though he of course was conscious of color. Because it was key for his safety to be so; and around whites, there was a certain way of talking and acting that Rodney was forced to adhere to. While not the South, it was nonetheless the era of Jim Crow America and our subject was surrounded by bias.

But he'd never had serious trouble. He was quiet, and his fantasies had left him little time to worry about racists and bigots. Because Rodney had been on a mission: both day and night, his only interest was studying fish and all things marine and aquatic.

And it was all because of Belle Isle. Because the same is just off the city; and back then, it had been home to a beautiful aquarium in addition to its flora and walkways. Now shut down, the aquarium was closed in the early 2000s because of a lack of funding.

But little Rodney had loved it. It was his Mecca, and his very first trip when he was eight-years-old had sparked his feverish daydreams. And the latter were truly febrile: always raging, they had set his youthful mind aflame while he'd pondered the sea and its contents.

Because how could you account for squids? And giant ones were astounding; but at the same time, the lesser ones that he'd seen in their tanks were nothing less than amazing. Moreover, it wasn't just squids but the sea as a whole that enthralled his passionate fancy.

And so he'd wished that the Rouge had marlins. It broke his heart, and the Detroit River was likewise devoid of creatures like dolphins and sea-crabs. Horribly polluted, all they could offer was mutated fish and trash such as condoms and beer cans.

But someday he would dive in the ocean. Because it was true that he'd loved Belle Isle; but nonetheless, he had wanted to be in the sea itself instead of just seeing exhibits. Like Jacques Cousteau, he would plunge to previously un-reached depths and chart their untold secrets.

And his mother had found him puzzling. Because when, she'd asked, would her child do more than just daydream? All he ever did was read about fish when he should have been doing his homework.

But she was pleased with Rodney's behavior. Soft-spoken, he had never gotten punished at school or ran with the wrong sort of children. And yet that was almost the problem: engrossed in books, he hadn't had a single friend with whom he could've gotten in trouble.

And his grades just had to get better. Because they'd paled beside his test scores; and every day, she had prayed that Rodney would go off to college and have a better life than her own. Poor and underpaid, she'd been working dead-end jobs since her husband had died when Rodney was only a toddler.

But she'd had a lesser concern though. Wherever he went, Rodney had sped like a bat out of hell while he'd ignored all cars and traffic. And it was because he was stuck in his daydreams: completely oblivious, he would tear down the street and his mother had feared that her child would get run over.

And there wasn't a reason he ran yet. Because it was something he naturally did then; and when they saw him, his neighbors had marveled at the breakneck clip at which he'd go running by them. With amused chuckles, they would watch him pass and more than one had said he was the next Jesse Owens.

But then one day he'd run into something that would change his life forever.

It was when he was twelve-years-old. And it was a summer day on Belle Isle; for as usual, he had gotten up and taken the bus to go see the aquarium's contents. Outside on a bench, he had left the exhibits and was thinking of the things that he'd lovingly just examined.

And so he hadn't heard them approach him. White and older, they were a group of teenagers who'd encircled the bench while Rodney gave in to his daydreams. And it was clear that they had been drinking: reeking of whiskey, they had surrounded Rodney before he looked up and saw that there was no one to help him.

"Are you lost?" one asked.

"Sir?" said Rodney.

"I just asked you if you're fucking lost or something."

"No," he'd practically whispered. "I'm not lost and I really don't want any trouble."

"Well then why are you here?" said another.

"I just came to see the aquarium."

"Then you are lost," said the first one. "Because a monkey like you belongs at the zoo and not the goddamn aquarium."

"But I just came to see the fish."

"Well we came to teach you a fucking lesson. Stay in your neighborhood with the other spooks and don't come back to Belle Isle."

And that's when they'd lunged at Rodney. But luckily, the latter had burst through a tiny gap and his pursuers chased him in vain.

And so Rodney had kept on running. For he would never forget what happened; and while unharmed, his body hadn't mirrored the murdered state of his cherished and deepest desires. Forsaken and dead, they had perished at the hands of those hostile boys who would haunt him both waking and dreaming.

Because everything was based upon color. He was crushed, and in his sorrow he'd assumed that every white was as bad as his drunken assailants. And hence why he'd gave up the ocean: as a black, he had felt like he could never explore the sea if he wasn't even allowed on Belle Isle.

And so Rodney had kept on running. But now he was aware of the reason; for as he sprinted, he'd remembered how the boys had howled with rage as their pursuit proved entirely futile. Filled with fury, he would run even faster as their phantom cries had re-echoed throughout his psyche.

Because he wasn't afraid of a scuffle. He was big, and every year his growing strength had made him just that more to handle. But running was better than fighting: as opposed to pain, shrieks of impotence and their accompanying shame were a sweeter and more vengeful music.

And his mother hadn't known why he'd altered. Utterly silent, he had never explained his disinterest in fish or why he was even more quiet. But something was the same and still vexed her: not high enough, his grades were mostly C's and D's as Rodney got ready for high school.

Yet then he had discovered his calling. And it happened in freshman gym class; for until then, Rodney had never actually played or shown any interest in football. Unsure of its rules, he had considered it to be a stupid game that was not only confusing but senseless.

But he'd known to run to the end-zone. On a kick-off in class, he had scampered with the ball for sixty-odd yards while his classmates had lagged behind him. And he'd left them breathless and panting: not even close, they'd failed to so much as touch his shirt as he rocketed past for a touchdown.

"Jesus Christ," said his teacher. Because he also coached for the high school; and after that play, he'd known at once that the Lewis kid was truly something special. "Shit," he'd happily thought. "With that sort of speed that fucking kid could be an all-American."

But Rodney had refused to listen. He was stubborn, and it was only the coach's heated insistence that eventually got him to practice. But then he'd learned something unusual: to his shock, Rodney had found out that he truly loved to play the game of football.

Because it was like being chased by those bigots. And he'd derived the same satisfaction; for when he scored, he had re-experienced the same sensation that he'd felt that day on Belle Isle. A spiteful blur, he had exulted when defenders couldn't ensnare him and harm his fleeing person.

And so Rodney had kept on running. But unlike before, it was with a football and the city's reporters were starting to come watch his high school. Because the Lewis kid was a phenom: a freshman on varsity, he had dazzled fans with a speed and strength that 'til then had never been witnessed.

And as a junior he was already a legend. But then he'd reached god-like proportions; for that year, his school had reached the city finals and cruised behind his performance. In pouring rain, he had rushed for over three hundred yards while also scoring six touchdowns.

"The game," said the *News*, "was played in a torrential downpour. But the only lightning to be seen on the field was the amazing 'Lightning' Lewis." And so thus was 'Lightning' created: no longer Rodney, he was called that name by everyone except for his censorious mother.

But there was one thing she liked about football. Because colleges were calling like crazy; and every day, when she went outside to get their mail there were letters from across the country. Desperately written, they had begged for Lightning to come to schools where his grades alone would have barred him.

And he didn't care who he signed with. Just wanting to play, he was fine with going to any school as long as they would allow him to do so. But his choice came down to two places: U of M and Ohio State, which had recruited Lightning the hardest.

Because they couldn't afford to lose him. And it was due to them being arch-rivals; for when they played, whoever got him would probably win when they annually met in November. Foaming at the mouth, their respective recruiters had praised their school colors while trying to get his commitment.

"The scarlet and grey," gushed Ohio. They were near tears, and 'maize and blue' had made Michigan's coaches just as choked-up and impassioned. But to Lightning they were both being silly: in his experience, the only colors that mattered at all were clearly black and white.

But his mother had a definite leaning. Because for her it was about academics; and accordingly, given that Michigan is so much better the decision for her was a plain one. A sensible woman, she had convinced her son to get a real education instead of just wearing a jock-strap.

And so Lightning had kept on running. In maize and blue, he'd awed the Big House while a hundred thousand had gaped at his staggering prowess. For it seemed like nothing could slow him: though in college, he was just as adept at gaining yards despite facing better opponents.

And the same was clear from the get-go. Because he'd made his debut in September; and on the first snap, he'd taken the ball as they played Wisconsin for seventy yards and a touchdown. An electrifying run, it had merely presaged the hundred more yards that he'd got through the course of the contest.

But Lightning was just getting started. Throughout the year, he had only improved while his overmatched foes were burned by his feinting and sprinting. Because at best they could hope to contain him: weaker and slower, they would sigh with relief if he burst for five yards as opposed to a fifty-yard touchdown.

And he'd been thrust in the national spotlight. Because his team was ranked first in the country; and by November, there was talk of Lightning winning the Heisman when he mauled Notre Dame and Purdue. Already the favorite, he'd helped his chances when he embarrassed the Spartans with two hundred yards in East Lansing.

But he'd still had to beat up the Buckeyes. It was the final game, and Michigan had made the trip to Columbus to face their most bitter of rivals. And Ohio was dreading the outcome: afraid of Lightning, they were wearing gray pants that some later said had stains of a curious brown.

Yet a miracle had delivered Ohio. Because his cleat got stuck in the turf there; and in a split second, Lightning was turned into Rodney forever when a helmet crashed into his knee-cap.

Because a cripple couldn't be 'Lightning'. And that's what the helmet had made him; for when it struck, it's angle of impact and massive force had reduced his right knee to tatters. Wholly destroyed, it was a jumble of tendons and shattered bones that would never really recover.

And Rodney had found it confusing. He was drugged up, and he couldn't grasp just what had happened on that fateful day in the Horseshoe. Because he'd seen a path to the end-zone: just to his left, he was about to make a simple cut when his cleats and the turf betrayed him.

But at least he was able to walk still. Because he'd needed four operations; and even then, it was incredibly painful and his useless right leg had changed his stride to a shuffle. Grotesquely, his ruined appendage had trailed his frame like defenders had once trailed Lightning.

And his career of course had been over. He'd never heal, and was now so slow that stooped old men would pass him by as he hobbled. For such was the extent of the damage: permanent and terrible, it had left him capable of nothing more than a halting locomotion.

"What a shame," said his former coaches. Because they'd known how much he loved football; and afterwards, with his ensuing depression he'd dropped out of school despite having free tuition. In utter despair, he'd gone from the champ of the forty-yard dash to the champ of dashing down forties.

And his mother had wanted him home. She'd begged, and was increasingly alarmed by what she could tell was his obvious problem with drinking. But Rodney refused to move back there: ashamed and obstinate, he was too embarrassed to limp on the streets that he'd rocketed down as a child.

But it wasn't as bad in Ann Arbor. For his reign there had been so fleeting; and as he stayed, he had worked odd jobs for the athletic department while his name was quickly forgotten. A gimpy nobody, he was barely recognized by anyone in town just five years after his glory.

And yet Rodney had still remembered. He'd yearned to play, and had further recalled that day on Belle Isle when he'd been attacked by those racists. And he would see the latter when sleeping: almost every night, they would assail him again in some monstrous from while Rodney was unable to flee them.

Because he was crippled even when dreaming. And before long they'd become one creature; for as he screamed, a giant form would chase him down and devour his helpless body. A hooded wraith, it had cloaked its face and savagely struck while Rodney fell into its clutches.

And hence why he would wake up shaking. He'd be sweating, and could never manage to fall back asleep while he had thought of the figure that stalked him. Or unless he had something to drink then: at four a.m., he would slam whatever booze that still remained from before he'd passed out for the evening.

And so Rodney had kept on drinking. Because he'd sip from a flask while working; and once off, he would limp to the bar before going back home and having even more drinks there. A raging drunk, he'd explored the depths of bottles of gin like he'd dreamed of exploring the ocean.

But one thing had kept him together. It was his mother, and once a month he had boarded a bus and gone to her house in the city. But then even she was taken: in the late 70s, Rodney's mother had simply dropped dead while she talked on the phone to a neighbor.

And so Rodney had kept on drinking. But now it was with total abandon; and after she died, he had lost his job because he'd been so drunk that he passed out when he was working. An unemployed cripple, he had likewise lost his rented room when he therefore couldn't afford it.

But to Rodney it hadn't mattered. Nothing had, and before too long he was sleeping outdoors and imploring people for quarters. And his sleep was even more fitful: as he dozed outside, the hooded figure would menace his dreams while always concealing its visage.

Yet then its face was un-muffled. And Rodney's horror was heightened; for when he saw it, it was the grayish void of nothingness to which our subject had sunken. Pathetically, his attempts to escape it by drinking more booze had hastened his rapid negation.

And so Rodney had kept on drinking. He drank all day, and had asked for change on Ann Arbor's streets as he'd strove to feed his addiction. And by now he resembled a scarecrow: barely eating, he had hovered around a hundred pounds when he used to weigh one-eighty.

But his decline had gone even further. Because he'd been homeless for over a decade; and half-crazy, he had started seeing the hooded figure sometimes even when waking. To his dismay, it had made the leap from his tortured dreams to his gin-and-forty-soaked hours.

"Fuck you," he'd hiss at his stalker. For to Rodney it was wholly lifelike; and when he saw it, he would stand on the street in the middle of the day and shriek at his phantom pursuer. An unrecognized bum, he had cursed and sworn while his former fans had anxiously gone walking past him.

And then there came the final dash of the amazing 'Lightning' Lewis.

It was two decades after his glory. A Saturday morning, the weather that day was atypically nice for Ann Arbor in late November. And Rodney had gotten up early: already drunk, he had gladly seen no sign of his wraith and was surprised there were so many people.

Because the thoroughfares were congested. And it showed just how far he'd fallen; for as he panhandled, he had no idea that the sea of people were all in town to watch football. Ironically, Michigan was playing Ohio State in the stadium that had once been his temple.

But he'd known that he wanted a forty. He was thirsty, and as he'd followed the crowd he was asking for change while they streamed their way to the Big House. But then he'd stopped by a lawn there: as he looked around, he'd noticed that a tailgater hadn't locked her car and that her purse was there for the taking.

And Rodney had taken two twenties. Because that was all that was in there; and as he limped off, he'd realized too late that there were a couple of fans who were sitting in a nearby Taurus. Smoking a joint, they'd put it out when they saw his theft and had started after poor Rodney.

But for a second it hadn't mattered. He was Lightning, and in his ravaged condition his final thought was that no living creature could catch him. Because that's when Rodney had perished: in front of the Big House, he had died of a massive heart attack brought on by the strain of fleeing.

And in a way he'd even been right. Having caught him, death itself was the only thing that could have stopped him when he was 'Lightning'.

. . .

James Curtiss *is a professional bass player who resides in Ann Arbor, Michigan. A graduate of U of M, he is a voracious reader who hates Ohio State and loves his alma mater. The latter provided him with a degree in history that he's never come close to using.*

Freeing Me
by Benjamin Grossman

I come from the walls
Triangles and sticks
My mother had no breasts
So I fed off myself
Long before I lost my father's name

From the beginning I stood on my feet
Learned what bullshit was
From reading classic books

I neglect history
Have made enough of my own

I am the first and last of my kind
Not a monkey man
But a man of the mind
Fragments are the answer to slowing time
And if you survive a thousand falls
You'll evolve into what I am

The inhuman voice
From a different age
Past and future fused
The philosopher sage

I hear colors
Smell words
Touch feelings
Taste sounds

I am what the ancients called clown
A master of oral lore
Heartless but undamaged
Ruined but remade
Logic intensified

I came from the walls
But my fall was from the clouds

. . .

Benjamin Grossman *received his MFA in Creative Writing from Rosemont College. He has previously written for flashfiction.net. Currently, he blogs about the crumbling existence of taboo at thebreakdownoftaboo.wordpress.com. He lives just outside of Philadelphia.*

Winter's Cinema

by Roman Colombo

The theater would not go dark for another few minutes. For now, I could take in all the details, hoping that they would help me if I needed to make a run for it. I've done this a dozen times now—exchanging information in the darkness of a Cineplex, a folder passing over the armrest between two seats from an anonymous deliverer sitting behind. I arrived first, they left first. They sat behind me. The same rules every time.

What has me so nervous is the movie itself. I know it's always random, but the fact that the drop is during a superhero movie scares the hell out of me. Action movies mean explosions. Explosions mean loud noises. The only thought going through my mind is that it's hard to hear a silencer during an explosion underlined by a bombastic score. I'm going to die while everyone cheers for the death on screen. Is it too much to ask for a death without irony?

As the lights settle, I mark a second issue...I am the only patron here. Why aren't there more people? Even a show time in the middle of the day will get a scattering of people. But I am completely alone. My hands grip the armrests, but I try to look calm. But since I am alone, I can't decide why I am trying to keep a straight face.

The trailer ends and the theater gets even darker. I hear nothing for a moment, see nothing. I nearly jump when the studio credits begin. I allow myself some nervous laughter. I'm getting ahead of myself. The other guy hasn't even arrived yet.

"You didn't silence your cell phone."

Or maybe he has. Stay calm. Don't turn around. Another rule—never turn around. I take out my cell phone and keep pressing the volume down button until it changes to "silent."

"That is hardly enough. Sure we might not hear the phone ring or even the vibration, but the signal itself if someone were to call or send you a message interferes with the speaker system in the auditorium. Minute though it may be, it will disrupt the cinematic experience—and we don't want any disruptions, do we, Mr. Reynolds?"

They've never said my name before—why does he know my name? Why is he using it?

"No, no disruptions." I reply.

"Good! I am glad we can see eye-to-eye, metaphorically speaking of course. We both know the rules of this game and should play our parts respectively. So, Mr. Reynolds, let us face forward in the manor of two movie patrons enjoying this fine film and conduct our business promptly."

I nod. "Why do you know my name?"

I hear him shift slightly. "That must be very disconcerting; to hear your name spoken in this setting, with the sort of business we conduct. I imagine that with every potential moment of action on the screen, a part of you is ready to flinch. Images of bullets tearing through your neck and lodging into the back of the chair in front of you are more vivid that what is happening on the screen. I would offer you my name, but I doubt it would calm your nerves."

I can't help it. "What is your name?"

"But you already know my name, don't you, Mr. Reynolds. I am the boogey man, the myth. I am the one they send when something is wrong. When someone breaks the laws amongst the lawless. An officer of injustice. You've heard my name in those circles before, haven't you? Tell me, what name do they say?"

My mouth is dry, but I manage to say "The Winter Saint."

He shifts again, and I can hear him even closer, talking directly behind me. "Why do you think that Mr. Grotto would send the Winter Saint for such a menial task, Mr. Reynolds? Why do you think I am here?"

I try to stop my voice from cracking, but it makes it even worse. "I was skimming from the payments. Tell Mr. Grotto that I'll pay it all back—with interest. I just needed the money for—"

"We know about the child support. Your children will be well provided for, I promise. Samuel Grotto has an excellent bereavement plan for all of his employees. Do not concern yourself; they will not miss their father's death."

"Please..."

Move your head for inches to the left, if you will."

I move my head, trying to think of anything I can do to persuade the Winter Saint not to kill me. But I have never heard the words "Winter Saint" and "let live" in the same sentence before. Hell, I've never *not* heard "Winter Saint" and "killed" in the same breath .

"Have you seen this movie yet?"

I look back at the screen. It is blurry for a moment—I realize that I am crying and dry my eyes. A large man in a weird mask is hanging from a cord, another guy clinging on to him. Below them, a torn apart plane crashes to the ground and erupts in flames. A hot flash grazes the right side of my neck, singing the skin. I hear a *thuck!* and feels little bits of plastic fall on my foot. It's bright enough to see the bullet now lodged into the seatback, hot enough to instantly melt the plastic around it. I'm waiting for that moment when I realize my windpipe is destroyed, but instead I am able to take a deep breath. The only pain I feel is the burn on the side of my neck. A bullet so carefully placed that it burnt the skin without breaking it.

A folder is passed between the seats, onto the arm rest. I take it and open it, looking down at a passport, driver's license, plane tickets, and a lease to an apartment.

"As far as Grotto is concerned, you died in that seat. You are gone. Let me make one thing perfectly clear: you are never to speak to your children again. If you do, I will kill them myself. From this moment on, you have a new name and a new life. You are never to contact anyone you have worked with or have known for the last however many years of your life. You live in Seattle Washington, and your plane leaves 2 hours after this movie ends. The only asterisk to the previous rule is that at some point, I may contact you and you are to do whatever I ask. Is this clear?"

I nod.

"Would you like a carbonated beverage?"

I hesitate, trying to figure out what he's talking about, but nod again. A large drink with a straw coming out of it appears to my right. I take it and start gulping it down. After several minutes of silence, I brave myself enough to turn around.

The Winter Saint was already gone.

• • •

Habemus Papam
by Kenneth Hickey

Brittle like glass when the news came, tiny pieces of wood splintering in towards the emptiness without name, back again from it hidings, under the bed at best guess, where all the monsters live, rental of the cupboard too expensive, especially with the extra tariff for leaving the door ajar included.

Hollowness, that happily hunts for these stumbling moments, here now, when the day stands still, the hissing of the passing traffic infinite, sloshing its way through the mortal remains of another unwanted spring shower. Hope the farmers are happy, it's not as if they ask for a lot.

And so much silence, now it's superfluous, repulsive laziness, loitering in corners of the room, would give my inner ear drum for a beating to fill the abyss with suffering screams.

But little so easy in this sheltered life. They tell us we've never had it so good, and they should know, the whispers say. They've always known, since the start.

And so it is, with words deserted, you find our subject, the one always thought so clever and so quick. What to say now, with the question marks in bubble clouds floating overhead. Half comprehended concepts, rotting paperbacks, depositions stolen from purveyors of the finest shining alchemies (owners dead or dying), lie dry humping at my feet, articulated impotence, gnawing on the weaker ones till nothing remains.

Words my thankless donkey, braying stupid as the crumbling clauses climb crapping from my mouth. Nothing to be said, a cop out, just too weak, too plain, too dumb, too cancerously cerebral for the interchange we engaged in.

And your message tripping through the air, asking if I'm alright.

The day we witnessed your sickness.

The fear that brought.

The weekend when the holy father went to see his boss.

• • •

Kenneth Hickey *was born in 1975 in Cobh. He has been published in Ireland, the UK and the United States. His writing for theatre has been performed in Ireland, the UK, New York and Paris. He has won the Eamon Keane Full Length Play Award as well as being shortlisted for The PJ O'Connor Award and the Tony Doyle Bursary.*

Snarling Metal
by Michael Plesset

Snarling metal looks at us strangely
could be hostile or only inanimate as clouds
of doubt roll around us surrounding
in a comforting way like the
embrace of a teacher who's approved
by the state, yesterday's
humor now fails, fresh
things needed daily, people
do die of boredom fresh
people fresh weather nerve wracking
fads like yoga stifle with
inappropriate clothes luckily
days get shorter exact change
is appreciated it's like breaking
even with the universe against
all odds.

• • •

Michael Plesset *did undergraduate and graduate work in mathematics, philosophy, sociology and English literature, and attended seminary at one time. He has published poetry, flash fiction and non-fiction articles. He has worked in the space program and the computer industry, wrote material for a stand-up comedian, and has taught English to Chinese students for the last 10 years.*

Glimmer

by Patrick Jackson

The thin gown hung just above his knobby knees and crinkled whenever he adjusted his weight. He wore a content smile on his face, as if he were a baby and had just relieved himself. For all Thelma knew, he just might have. She knew he was in there. This was a trick, a farce, a game. Bernard wasn't trying hard enough, he was letting the illness win. When Thelma looked into his blue eyes, they would glimmer back at her as if she was in on the joke. But she wasn't.

"I'm sorry," the doctor said, holding a clipboard and talking to Thelma as if she were the only one in the room. "He's only going to get worse. Have you considered looking into a senior memory care community?"

"That's not an option," Thelma said, standing and pulling her purse over her shoulder. "Get changed, Bernard. We're leaving."

The doctor raised his eyebrows before scribbling something on the notepad. Then, he left.

Two years passed since they had last seen the inside of a medical office. Thelma was proud of this. She sat next to Bernard on the couch, watching a news program. News used to be Bernard's favorite; he would get all excited over something that was said and on more than one occasion could be seen yelling and cursing the anchorman on television as if he was arguing with him. But those days are long gone and Thelma looked over at Bernard who stared at the screen, his mouth slightly open and his hands placed calmly in his lap. The program is half over when Thelma begins to smell a sickly sour scent coming from her husband's direction. At first she thinks it's just gas, but when the smell doesn't dissipate, she realizes exactly what it is.

"Oh, Bernard!" she cries. "You've wet yourself again! And right on the couch. Come on." She grabs his hand and pulls him up, exposing the dark stain underneath him.

"I didn't know I had to go," he says, not embarrassed but almost with a sense of amusement. His lips begin to curl upwards in a smile.

"You think this is funny?" Thelma asks, yanking him to the bathroom. "Why don't you clean it, then?" She slams the door and stands out in the hallway. Despite the numerous doctors that told her what to expect and the literature she read with informative titles like 'What do to when your loved one has Alzheimer's', she still cannot believe that this man – who once was the president of a small organic food distributor, could easily explain the stock market with all its intricacies, and would read the New York Times from cover to cover every morning over breakfast – could now not even realize when he had to take a piss.

Thelma storms off to the kitchen and fills a small plastic bucket with hot water and Lysol, the lemony scent so strong it provides a slight tingle in her nose. After grabbing a sponge, she returns to the dark spot. "Ugh," she groans as she slowly gets down on her knees and begins to scrub.

They just finished lunch and Bernard managed to wear the majority of the tomato sauce so that the front of his shirt looked as if he just returned from the butchers. Thelma takes his plate, shaking her head at the mess. The ground underneath his chair is littered with breadcrumbs. "Gracie!" Thelma calls. An easy fix. She just doesn't have the energy today to clean up. "Gracie!" She listens for the clipping sound of the small longhaired Jack Russell's claws against the tile, but there is nothing. "Where's the dog?" Thelma asks, not really expecting a response. "Bernard. Where is the dog?"

He smiles back at her, the son of a bitch. Worthless. She brushes past him and continues to walk around the house, calling the dog. "Gracie! Gracie! Where are you?" Silence. She walks back to the living room and down the hallway into one of the three guest bedrooms, listening for something, anything. Then she hears it as she passes the sunroom that has two of the three long windows open allowing the cool spring air to enter the house. It's faint, but she's sure it's Gracie barking. "Gracie," she says. And she's off, rushing - as fast as a person with a hip replacement and surgery on their right knee over four times can rush – out the front door and onto their great expanse of a lawn. The barking is louder now, yet still so far off. "Grace!" she calls, "Come!" The barking begins to fade and she thinks about getting in her car to find the dog. She absolutely cannot allow Gracie to run off. Who knows what she may encounter out in the woods behind their house. Why, just the other week the neighbors said they may or may not have seen a bear! She doesn't dare imagine what might be lurking out there. She turns and begins walking back to the front door, past the overgrown beds of flowers that used to flourish and be the cause of envy of their neighbors. That was Bernard's job, and he took much pride in it. On any given day, he could be seen on his knees, his hands lost within the rich soil beneath the vibrant reds and yellows, and greens, his neck a sore red from the sun. Thelma shakes her head as if trying to physically rid herself of the memories and makes her way back inside to search for her keys.

"Bernard," she says loudly because he is no longer in the kitchen. She rifles through her purse on the kitchen counter. "I have to go out to find Gracie. Did you let her out?" She finds the keys. "If anything happens to Gracie, I don't know what I'll do," she says. Her hands are shaking more than usual. "You hear me, Bernard? I know you hear me!" Just as she turns to the corner to head out the door to the garage where their Lincoln Town car is parked, Bernard steps from seemingly out of nowhere and directly into her path.

"Oh!" Thelma cries, and staggers backwards. Bernard – whether aware of it or not – picks a perfect opportunity of Thelma's backward trajectory and places both hands on her shoulders and gives a helpful push - not too hard, but almost as if he were swinging his grandchild on a swing. The push is enough to send the already spiraling Thelma back a couple more steps and that's when she hears the sickening sound of the hip giving way - or maybe the knee - whichever one, the sound alone is enough for her to go down. Hard. "Aggh!"

she screams as she hits the hard marble floor and then it is all black.

The marble feels cool against her cheek. Thelma tries to sit up and is hit with a throbbing pain in her side that quickly seems to extend to every inch of her body. She lies back down and stares at the ceiling, holding back tears. "Bernard!" she cries out, her voice slightly hoarse. How long has she been unconscious? An hour, at the most? "Bernard!"

It is quiet. She notices a bulge in the white paint on the ceiling. Must be a leak or something that caused it. She stares at it for so long she swears it begins to pulse. Bernard is nowhere to be found. He's probably enjoying this, the bastard, she thinks. It isn't until her eyes begin to drift shut that she hears the familiar shuffling coming her way. She glances to her left and sees the tattered brown slippers pointed at her.

"Bernard, thank goodness," she says. "Call 911, sweetie. Or hand me my phone. I think it's on the kitchen counter." No response. "Bernard, honey, I am *hurt!*"

Bernard shuffles a little closer. She cannot twist her head the right way to see him just yet, but what she does see - like a snake emerging from the grass - is a brown slipper slowly coming towards her.

"What are you doing?" she asks. The slipper makes contact with her side, pushing in the soft flesh. "Ow!" Thelma cries out, causing Bernard to give a little yelp of surprise before retracting the slipper and galloping out of the room.

"Goddammit!" Thelma yells, then begins to sob.

She must have fallen asleep for when she wakes only a faint orange glow cuts through the window and onto the marble floor making it shine as if lit from beneath it. She tries to turn on her side, but the pain is so severe that she is afraid any more movement may cause her to black out completely. "Help!" she yells, but her voice has lost its gusto. If only she had a glass of water.

He's doing this on purpose, she thinks. I just know he is. Getting back at me the only way he can. Those doctors, what do they know? They don't see him, see the way he looks at things. I know he's there, he's just trying to fool me. Well, he's fooled them, but he won't fool me.

"Bernard!" she yells again. Thelma holds her breath, listening for anything, but the house sounds empty. "Ohhhhh," she moans before allowing more tears to stream down her cracked cheeks. Her whole left side has become numb and her mouth is now almost completely dry.

In a couple more hours or less, nighttime will arrive and Thelma will be immersed in darkness. She turns her head to try to lean on the other side, and when she does she sees the brown slippers staring right back at her.

"Bernard?" she asks, looking up. She now sees him in his entirety. Bernard is no longer Bernard. As if seizing the opportunity to go fully insane, he towers over Thelma. He is shirtless, his chest hollow and thick with curly white hairs. There is also a large dark stain down the crotch of his jeans that continues down the middle pant leg, and his thick blondish-grey hair is spiked at all odd angles as if he has been wrestling with someone or something. But while these things all frighten Thelma to some extent, it is the look on his face that seems to strip away her breath – his eyes are distant, as if he is somewhere else entirely and not standing in the kitchen looking down upon the crumpled form of his wife of 30 years. And with his bushy grey eyebrows contorted down towards the center of his nose he looks, well, angry.

"Honey, please," she begs, her eyes tearing up. "I need help."

For a moment, his face slackens and his head slightly tilts to the side, like a puppy hearing a strange noise for the first time, but just as quickly his face darkens again. She watches as he pulls back a foot as if ready to punt a football, and swings it forward, catching her right in her soft midsection so that when his foot makes contact a deep groan she didn't know she was capable of making spews forth. He turns and strolls away.

When she awakens, she sees an ant, no bigger than a decent sized crumb crawling near her face. She watches its mini antennas search the air, twitching sporadically before rubbing them together and zigzagging away until it's out of sight. She wonders if this is the last image she will see – an ant – and if so how disappointing that would be. She is worried because the pain in her hip, her knee, everywhere, has dissipated. I'm going into shock, she thinks.

On top of that, her mouth is dry. Extremely dry. She slides her tongue across her lips, feeling the indentations of the cracks like dried out riverbeds in the bottom of a canyon. A coppery taste remains on her tongue and she knows it is blood. She's also pretty sure she has wet herself – she smelled it an hour ago but since then she must've gotten used to it because she doesn't smell anything anymore. The clock in the hallway chimes, and she counts it out. It is now four in the morning. She has been lying on the ground for a solid 12 hours. 12 hours! She's about to cry again, but doesn't have the energy. Instead her face remains twisted, wanting to cry but out of tears. This is it, she thinks. This is where I am going to die. She doesn't want to admit it, but she's utterly petrified of death. There were so many things she still wanted to do, but with Bernard getting sick and all, she had to put them all on hold. She imagined her retired life being so much more than her working one – though she didn't have much of a working life, Bernard wanted her at home with the kids. But when Bernard retired, and seeing how their bank account seemed to just keep growing and almost take on a life of its own, she believed they would make use of that money. She wanted to go to Ireland, where her parents had immigrated from, and meet her distant ancestors. She wanted to see the pyramids and perhaps even ride on the back of a camel. She wanted to take cruises, long cruises out into the middle of the ocean. She so very badly wanted to step out onto the deck at twilight and see if it were really true that the stars seemed to melt right back into the ocean if you go out far enough. There were so many things she wanted to do, that she thought she was going to do. It was Bernard that ruined it all. The disease did not only take his life away, but it took Thelma's along with it.

At around 7 in the morning - at least she thinks it is 7 - the sunlight hit the room bringing with it the young energy that only morning light has. Her left side was now completely numb, and when she pulled her pants down slightly to examine the extent of the damage, her skin above her hip had turned a dangerous darkened blue, violent almost. She had a dream Bernard was out there, helping her up, giving her a glass of water, conversing with her, but when she awoke her mouth was still dry and she knew it was just her imagination.

She had accepted her fate so that when Bernard came back into the room, still looking like a castaway on a deserted island, she didn't even say a word. Tilting her head, she looked up at him.

There was something different about him. He looked...there.

"Bernard?" she says. All she wanted – all she needed – was him to say something, a moment no matter how brief of cognizance so that he could realize how much trouble she was in, how she was going to die unless something was done.

Before she allowed her eyes to shut, she regarded her husband one final time. She saw a glimmer of lucidity in his eyes, like a coin catching the sunlight off in the distance. And as he looked down upon her crumpled form, she swore she saw him smile.

• • •

Patrick Jackson *is a graduate from the MFA program in Creative Writing at Fairleigh Dickinson University. He grew up in the small town of Lancaster, Pennsylvania. After graduating college, Patrick moved to New York City, where he has lived for the past 8 years. He teaches and tutors writing for several different SUNY colleges.*
He has been published in The Grey Sparrow, The Cynic Online Magazine, and The Cracked Spine.

A Tiger By The Tale
by Gary Clifton

Brooks Chadsey, a rather aimless farm kid from rural Texas, joined the Army on graduation from high school in 1969. Assigned to the elite 101st Airborne, he was sent to Viet Nam.

During a mission in a driving rainstorm northwest of Pleiku, near the Cambodian border, he stumbled across a young tiger trapped by its tail beneath a tree felled by the storm. The animal struggled and screamed piteously and was unable to chew himself loose because the tree had partially landed on his hips.

Brooks studied the catastrophe. Initially he decided to shoot the wretched creature, but gunfire would alert the enemy. Brooks found a stout tree limb. Slinging his rifle over a shoulder in case the animal attacked, put his full weight to prying the tiger free.

The tree gave way, the animal struggled clear, and Brooks froze, his rifle at alert if the animal turned on him. In the rainy mist, Brooks was astounded to see what he interpreted as gratitude in the animal's eyes. The tiger limped away, stopped several yards away, and clumsily raised a paw in what could only be a salute. Then the magnificent creature disappeared into the thick vegetation, his mangled tail dragging behind.

Brooks survived Viet Nam and eventually earned a PhD. in Animal Science specializing in habits and behavior of big cats. His work earned him a tenured faculty position at a major east coast university. He became famous among his peers.

The circus came to town. Specifically to see the treatment of large cats in circus custody, Brooks treated two of his star pupils to an afternoon at the big top. They quietly worked their way to the rear holding area where three large, beautiful tigers were confined in wheeled cages.

Two of the creatures were young, but the third was old. To Brook's astonishment, its tail had been mutilated and hung straight down. Then, miracles of miracles, the tiger fixed its gaze on Brooks, the same grateful, loving gaze he'd seen from the animal he'd saved twenty years before. Brooks instantly knew the bond - it was the animal from Viet Nam!

Brooks slipped under the rope barricade and sprang up onto the ledge outside the heavy bars of the cage. "Good God, Dr. Chadsey, stop!" shouted one of the students. But the tiger turned sideways to the bars. Brooks reached through and stroked the giant back like one would pet a housecat. He patted the animal's neck, then slid his hand to touch the maimed spot where his tail had been ruined.

The tiger snatched Brook's arm, tore it off at the shoulder and calmly sprawled on the cage floor gnawing on the twitching delicacy.

Brooks lay dead of traumatic shock and blood-loss beneath a sheet. His students stood-by, distraught.

"Hell, ol' Barney was born in captivity." the keeper said. "Roun' ten years ago, got his tail smashed in the cage door."

"Mistaken tiger identity, suspect already in custody," the cop jotted in his notebook.

• • •

Gary Clifton, *forty years a cop, has over forty short fiction pieces published or pending with online sites, Clifton has been shot at, shot, stabbed, sued, lied to, and often misunderstood. He is currently out to pasture on a dusty north Texas ranch and doesn't much care if school keeps or not. He has an M.S. from Abilene Christian University.*

Closer Than the Other Side of the World

by David Seguin

Mindy wanted to be home, back in Iowa, but was stranded in the Bangkok airport. Street filling rain closed the airport, along with dizzying winds and lightning thrusts from the latest tropical storm; nobody was leaving anytime soon. She tried to sleep on a bench and shut out the chaos of thousands of traveling strangers. Startled by the incomprehensible ranting of a woman's voice, Mindy focused her tired eyes on the feet behind her bench. A pair of shiny brown loafers faced off with a set of five inch heels. The voice intensified every time the maroon leather shoes moved toward the loafers. Leopard print could be seen peeking out between the screaming toes. Mindy closed her eyes but the yelling continued to disturb her. "You better tell her!" were the first English words Mindy comprehended, angry words in Thai followed for emphasis. The Thai woman continued, even louder this time, "I'm number one wife. I should be only wife. You love me? You fix!" The escalating conversation prevented Mindy from sleeping. Two pairs of children's shoes, one blue and one purple, scurried around and in between the adult shoes, occasionally bumping the vertical rolling suitcase. A man's voice comforted the children, and then the woman said "Don't talk me again until done. You come home to me." The brown loafers shuffled closer to the heels, "I'm sorry. I'm going to do it. I promise. I'll be back home with you and the kids next week. I love you." The shoes all came together then turned their separate ways and flew apart as if they were repelling magnets. Mindy closed her eyes again, searching for more sleep. Her parents last message online reassured her saying, *this too would pass*.

With the shoe assault gone, the man walked in repeated loops around Mindy's bench-bed. Her body looked like the covered mound of a freshly buried grave, her hosed off canvas jacket hid her like a tarp. She heard his shoes shuffle as he reversed direction. Her eyes opened and saw his brown loafers still lingering, disrupting the light pattern reaching her face from under the bench. The fake light produced an iridescent glow not generated by the sun. Natural light was still hours away. The man finally claimed the seat at the end of the bench, next to Mindy's dingy sock covered feet. Her head, braced by her large backpack and hidden by her long brown unwashed hair, faced the back of the bench, away from the chaos. Mindy presented less risk of disruption despite her odor; she craved a shower that was still days away. She fantasized about the sleep she was not getting, about sleep in a real bed on a mattress with clean sheets.

About 4 A.M. a young boy pushed a teetering mountain of mismatched luggage into the airport. He navigated the entry and picked up speed as he steered the overflowing luggage cart towards Mindy's bench. Two adults trailed behind. They accelerated with screams and tried to stop the impact. The collision of bags into bench was enough to jolt Mindy awake. The sudden change caused her to kick the man at the end seat with her dirty socks. Rising sleepily from under her tarp blanket, she said, "I'm sorry. I didn't mean to kick you. Are you ok?"

"No problem, I'm fine. I was already awake. Just sitting here waiting."

Mindy smoothed back her shoulder length greasy hair, put on her mud stained baseball hat, pulled her shirt down, and her grimy socks up. She sat up and faced the stranger. Her mouth was disgusting; it was like licking the dirty airport floor with each breath. She dug through her backpack for some gum. The pack held enough for the month long trip, with some room to spare. It could hold most of a dead body if needed.

Her aide trip to Thailand was finally over. The devastation from the Thai flooding was far worse than she imagined, the online reports of *worst flood ever* were validated by what she saw. Even though the flooding occurred months ago there was plenty for her school mission group to do. The flooding went through every part of Thailand, Bangkok and rural areas were hit hard, both needed enormous amounts of help cleaning up, rebuilding, and trying to survive. Mindy's group worked in Ayutthaya province in the capital city of the same name. A little more than two hours by train, the city is actually an island created by three rivers. Basic services of running water and electricity had only recently been restored.

Mindy removed her phone from the pocket of her backpack. Twitter, Facebook, and every other online version of home was her main way to keep up with everyone back in Iowa, and to let them know about the work she was doing. Her friends should be finishing their Thursday. She was now capable of holding two time zones in her brain simultaneously; day is night, night is day.

'@mindymindy: Looks like 1 hour sleep is all I get. Up and at it in Thailand. Looking to get a flight home today'

The man offered Mindy some of his breakfast, an extra granola bar from the hotel.

"Thanks," she said. "It's been a rough night. I'm Mindy."

"Brendan, nice to meet you."

"You stuck here too?" She dug through her backpack for water.

"Yeah, it's a real mess. I fly back and forth every month. This is the worst delay I've seen. Usually it will just rain and rain but flights will keep going. This wind and lightning is not normal and could keep us here a while. How about you? Looks like you spent the night."

He looked at the Delta counter; the employees were just now arriving and setting up.

"I was here helping with Thai flood relief for the past month. Now I'm on my way home to Iowa. The rest of my group got out on a flight yesterday. I was last and didn't make it."

Mindy told Brendan about the Catholic mission organized by her high school. The mission put together a month long trip to help with the recovery from the Thai floods. The sights and accounts of real people on social media stayed with her during her senior year. She followed their struggles with the rising waters and destruction on a daily basis. It created a bond with her new remote friends, sympathy for their needs and the pain they were going through. The pictures of families escaping the waste high water with all their possessions on a raft or of homes completely washed away into the ocean drove her to seek out the mission opportunity. Mindy wanted to help; she wanted to do something. She spent the month repairing villages, rebuilding homes, shoveling river silt from living rooms, sorting through ruble to help find family photos, and anything anybody needed. Despite her exhaustion, she was proud of her decision to come to Thailand.

"It's amazing how small the world is now. Just like if the next town over had trouble, I was able to get over here and help people I've come to know online."

"Impressive, especially for someone so young. I know a lot of people impacted. I'm from Chicago but live here most of the time. Many of my relatives and friends have been struggling to get back to normal or even just to survive. Even my house suffered some damage and we are near Bangkok," he replied, and then glanced to the Delta counter where an employee was adjusting signs and organizing people into a snaking maze.

"Thanks, it felt really good to help."

"So you have a flight out yet?"

"Nope, I have been here overnight hoping to get on one. My original flight was canceled yesterday. Delta told me that it might be a few days. This rain and wind and the crazy lightning have me a little concerned they might be right. Not sure if I want to fly in this anyway."

"It's ok; I've flown out in much worse. The Delta counter will open at 5 A.M. I have a ton of miles and status; let me see what I can do. If nothing else you won't have to stand in the general travel line."

Holding her phone up towards Brendan, Mindy said, "Thanks. I keep updating my parents online. They feel helpless since there is nothing they can do but wait back in Iowa."

"I don't understand all that constantly connected online stuff, but I do understand parents missing their kids. My daughters tell me I'm old because I use email. Anyway, I'll see what I can do, let's hope it works out, for both of us."

Brendan was going to help her get on a flight. She would be home soon. Back to her phone she posted a few more pictures of the airport and shared the kindness of Brendan. She was making full use of the international mobile plan her parent's setup for her trip. They wanted to know she was safe, every day. Mindy's promised to keep status updates coming, with pictures, and call home at least once a day. The constant communication with family and friends helped her feel close from the other side of the world.

'@mindymindy: Nice guy in airport helping me get on a flight home. I might see Iowa this weekend after all.'

Mindy smiled when Brendan handed her the ticket. She had a confirmed seat on Delta 284, with Brendan, in Business Class. The flight was delayed, all flights were, but she would be on her way home, out of Bangkok soon. In addition, her ticket gave her access to the airline club, the shower would be the first with hot water since Iowa.

'@mindymindy: Traveling home in style, thanks to the generosity of a stranger. Confirmed on Delta 284 in a fancy bed seat! Pictures soon."

The first thing Mindy did when they reached the airline club was shower and change into fresh clothes. When she returned to Brendan he had already secured food, drinks and two seats in the corner by a window. She set her pack aside and lowered herself into the plush cushioned chair next to Brendan. The chair didn't recline, but was the most comfort she had sitting since she was back in her family room in Iowa with her parents. Mindy posted pictures of everything: the ticket with a single digit row number, her complimentary shower amenities kit, and her clean feet perched up near the window with storm clouds still hovering outside. The gloomy sky reluctantly allowed daylight to emerge but only with continued rain and lightning. Delays continued but she was comfortable. Mindy even posted a picture of her and Brendan. Seemed only fitting to show her parents and friends the man responsible for saving her from unknown days waiting on standby for a flight out of Bangkok.

"So what do you do in Bangkok?" asked Mindy.

"I work for a financial consulting firm. Been coming to Bangkok every month for the past six years. It's exhausting." Brendan switched to whisky now that another 2 hour delay had been announced.

"Wow, that sounds tough."

"Yes, it's not easy. It's hard to be away from family. My wife and kids dropped me off at the airport. We were having a little argument back there when she dropped me off. I'm sure the entire airport heard her. I think I'm going to have to make a change."

Mindy sipped Diet Coke and sorted through the snack array on the table. Brendan got more whiskey; he appeared agitated and nervous, like his brown loafers were still pacing back in the terminal.

Mindy asked, "Are you ok? Did I say something?" He paused, drank his new whiskey in one gulp and exchanged the empty for his backup full glass. He sat up straight and faced Mindy.

"So I guess this is as good a place as any to confess. I have been bad and have no way out. I am trying to do the right thing," said Brendan.

"Is this about the argument with your wife back at the terminal? She seemed angry." Mindy sat up in her chair. She sensed she might have to focus for this conversation.

"I think it would help me to explain the situation to you, to get it straight in my mind. And this storm looks like it still has some life left." The smell of whiskey traveled with every word spoken, giving each syllable importance and weight.

"Ok." She picked up one of the snack plates Brendan had put out for them.

"Well, no easy way to say it. You're right we were arguing and she is mad. The problem is I have two wives, actually two families. One lives in Thailand and the other lives in Chicago. I don't know how this happened, well I do but I let it continue."

Brendan spoke as if one of his wives were trying to listen in. Mindy tried not to move too much, tried not to ask questions. She listened intently as if she was in a review session for a test or getting directions to a party. How could someone get in this position, and stay there for years? She wanted to know.

Brendan said, "Seventeen years ago I married Marcy, my wife in Chicago. We went to college together and got pregnant and got married, in that order. Raven was born then we had another daughter, Violet, a few years later. I don't know how I could have done this to them but I have and I continue the lies." He shifted in his seat to face Mindy and looked into her eyes. Mindy felt uncomfortable with the change but understood the serious tone of the conversation; he was explaining his transgressions as if to his own daughters.

"That means they're close to my age." The stench of his whisky annoyed and lingered in Mindy's space.

"Yup, Raven is 18. She's a lot like you, adventurous and caring." Brendan paused, exchanged his drink from one hand to the other and pressed his head into his free hand. "So then I get this great promotion to work with our bank customers in Thailand. Trouble is I need to travel back and forth. I started to spend one month in Chicago and one month here in Bangkok. It was tough on me, Marcy too."

"I can't imagine being away for that long." Mindy added. Lightning continued to disrupt the sky. It became normal throughout their conversation, losing power to startle with each successive bolt. "It's going to be ok to fly through this storm right?"

"Yea, it'll be fine. They're going to delay until its safe. Anyway, in Thailand I met a girl, not sure why but I did. It was late, I was out and I should have just gone back to the hotel. She was young, I was lonely. We talked about our lives and shared stories growing up. We really connected. Before I knew it we had been together a few nights. It was supposed to be nothing more than that, a one time thing. I came back a few months later and found her again. She told me she was pregnant. Of course this has to happen to me."

"Not cool." Mindy said softly.

"When Hansa was four months pregnant, we visited her family. We spent a weekend together on the beaches in Phuket, southern Thailand. Have you been there? It has to be one of the most romantic places I've been. Perfect white sand met by turquoise water. You know all those pictures online and TV ads of exotic topical beach vacations? That's Phuket. I felt a connection I could not give up and married her. She knew all about my family in Chicago. We wanted to be together and figured we would work out the details later."

"Really, you married her?" Mindy wanted to lash out.

"Hansa and I are still married, five years now. We have Malee, our daughter who is five and yes we have a son too, Akkarat, he is four. I talked my company into paying my Thailand bonuses to a local account. It's enough for our little house outside Bangkok." Brendan took a deep breath.

"I can't believe this." How about he get a vasectomy and stop taking advantage of women? His words were starting to slur. Mindy was still processing the insanity, trying to get everything straight.

"I really do mean well. I am not trying to hurt anyone and I am going to fix it. Our argument back there was that I need to leave Marcy and the girls in Chicago. Hansa wants me to make a decision and stay in Thailand for good." he said. His words did not convince Mindy he was ready for that conversation. Brendan slouched back into the chair, staring out the window unmoved by the current flurry of wind and lightning.

"I just feel bad for both your families. It sounds like everyone is going to get hurt."

"I know. That's why I'm on my way to Chicago to end my marriage with Marcy. The girls are older and Hansa is right, I can't carry on like this. I want to be with Hansa. She's the one I love." Full of whiskey, Brendan's words had no spaces.

"So you will live in Thailand full time?"

"I know, I'm sorry Raven. I didn't mean to hurt any of you." Brendan hid his face in his hands. Mindy stared at him wondering if he really just called her by his daughter's name?

"It will be ok in the end. You are doing the right thing." Mindy tried to reassure from a distance. Brendan composed himself again filled with a few deep breaths.

"I don't know. This if really fucked up. I don't care about the house, cars, or the money. And Marcy will be fine eventually, even if she hates me. I don't want to lose my daughters; I just hope they can get past it someday. I hope it is not forever." He shook his head and took in the last of his drink.

Mindy slouched back in her chair. Brendan didn't deserve to have any family. Mindy considered him a loser but now the Chicago family could move on, without him. And the Thai family would have to find a way to live with him. She tried to think about what she would do if she was Raven or Violet. Her mind could not relate to multiple wives, divorce, and half siblings from another country. That wouldn't happen in Iowa. She wanted to update her parents, at least online, to feel close to them, to be reassured about the stability and truth of her own family structure.

Brendan stretched his legs and went to the restroom, Mindy went online and put out some updates, everyone back home would be asleep now but when they woke up the details would be waiting.

'@mindymindy: Wow, nice guy is loser. Two families! Unbelievable.'

'@mindymindy: Two wives, one in Chicago and one in Thailand. And 4 kids total.'

'@mindymindy: don't know, sort of feel sorry for him. But then I think of the kids and go back to thinking jerk'

'@mindymindy: he is going home this weekend to end it with the Chicago family.'

'@mindymindy: honey I'm home…oh by the way I have a Thai wife and two kids and I'm leaving you for them…goodbye.'

'@mindymindy: Storms still have us delayed. I don't even jump with lightning anymore. Brendan says it's safe to fly. Details later…'

'@mindymindy: on the flight, delta 284, looks like we are finally leaving. These seats are sweeeeeeeet! Thanks Brendan, good luck confessing to your Chicago family.'

Mindy posted one last comment with their picture from their seats.

'@mindymindy: Here we are, ready to take off. Looks like lightning stopped. Next tweet from Chicago!'

She read the menu while everyone else was boarding. She thanked Brendan again but he still seemed a little shaken. He became distant once the whiskey wore off. He had said only a few words to Mindy since the airline club and no longer looked at her. Maybe Brendan reevaluated his situation, or was regretted his confession to her, a stranger from Iowa. The buckle was tight and the seat was in the upright position. The captain apologized for the delay. There was a break in lightning and the wind had calmed enough to get out of Bangkok, if they hurried. The pilot warned the beginning would be bumpy until they cleared the threatening weather. Mindy saw the rain coming down undisturbed by wind or lightning, the sun never made it. They were off.

According to the official report, lightning struck the plane. Delta flight 284 was the top story on the evening news for days. *Tragic accident*, *search for the black box*, and finally *no survivors* were the headlines through the week. Questions were endless from Marcy, Raven and Violet but the result was still the same. Their doubts would not cancel their father's funeral today. The viewing started in an hour, followed by a service at the same funeral home. Everyone remained almost ready, as if staying in the house would change the result. Raven and Violet spent the morning annoying each other while their mother hid in her bedroom.

"Stop it Raven. What do you want?" said Violet.

"Look at the iPad, look at the picture!" Raven forced her sister's head into the glass.

"That's dad. Why are you showing me this? Why are you trying to upset me before the funeral?"

"I was doing Twitter searches for his flight that crashed, just to see what people were saying. I found this Mindy bitch talking about dad. She was on his flight."

"Don't torture me with this crap."

Raven took the iPad back and made a few swipes.

"Shut up. Read it, all the posts."

"Who is @mindymindy? And why do I care?" she asked, trying to look up. Raven shoved her head back down.

Violet gave in and read more of the posts. She wanted to know why @mindymindy had a picture of dad. Raven kept repeating, "I don't know." Violet wanted to know why the girl was calling their dad names and what all this had to do with a Thai family and four kids.

Raven took the iPad back, scrolled to the most disturbing Tweet. She read it again to be sure it was the right one. Then she read it to Violet.

"Now listen to this." Raven said. Violet shook her head, covered her ears, and rested her elbows on the table. Raven slapped her across the head and told her to listen. She read the Tweet about their dad leaving them. Hearing the words aloud made it real, for both sisters. Their dad was coming home to leave. He wanted to be with his Thai family.

"Girls, are you ready? We have to get to the funeral home, now. We're going to be late!" said Marcy. In an instant they turned off the screen and hurried to their mother, fighting back tears with closed mouths.

. . .

Masochism
by e.a.d. sellors

There's a comfort
to be found
in every torture

a hell in every
smile

be thankful
to the bastards
who try and break
our balls

it is best to be poor
in this world
to know how the world
treats its poor

the cheapest wine
tastes a million dollars
when you can't afford it

that's why there's only one way
to succeed in this life
and it comes from a deep
experience
of suffering.

. . .

Anarchy in the U.S.
by Paul Reilly

Benny was not an anarchist. He didn't need to tell himself that: plenty of other people had told him already. Jessica, Audrey, David, Pierce, Laurel, Dan K, Dan C, Dan R, Dan W, and Virginia all assured him of this fact.

"You're not an anarchist," David said near the end of September, when the movement began. They had both met Walden, but cigarettes and calzones were more pressing topics in their personal protest than the anarchist figurehead. Pierce walked into the tent five minutes later, armful of steaming pizza boxes, and no one thought of violence even once.

"You're not an anarchist," Pierce said on the porch in October the night when the air started to chill. His tone was very different from David's in September. The porch remained the same, but the way Pierce shook and spat made Benny uneasy. David sat quietly in a lawn chair in the corner with rapt, blank eyes. He casually twirled a crinkled leaf, one of many that fell on him from the passing gusts of faded reds, oranges, yellows, browns.

"You're not an anarchist," David said in November, with the most confusing tone yet. A more complicated reprimand, like a mother caught smoking from a stash of confiscated weed. This was the last thing David would say to Benny before donning a black hood and breaking from the crowd at Dewey Square, a jagged hunk of granite clutched in his hand with ragged idealism.

A lot changed since September, besides the tone of each identical statement. For one: Benny knew actual anarchists in October, whereas all he knew of anarchy in September was from interpretation, vague definition acquired by textbooks and friends of friends of friends.

In October, those definitions tightened. They constricted around the wobbly wooden porch, snuffing out a candle standing beside a tasteless mug, Pierce's, which read "#1 CAD." Tests necessitated a break from the occupation, so the whole crew settled at David's for the night. As expected, bringing that many young activists together in one cozy place, no matter how often they agree, was a bad idea. Though the debate started spirited, letting everyone from Virginia to the more reserved Dan K chime in, a thick cloud of cigarette smoke and hot air had suffocated all but Pierce and Benny.

"But I think I actually am," Benny said, "or maybe I'm becoming one. I find it harder every day to stand there in that throng, trying not to sneer and shout. Occupy is just another system disguised as a rebellion. It's flawed, limited, immobile, and guided by a hierarchy that no one wants to admit exists. We are suffocating any real progress with this illusion of democracy."

"Nobody said Occupy was perfect," Pierce said, leaning forward with a fiery spark, the thick thistle coating his cheeks and neck leaning forward with him, "But whatever bullshit these wackos are feeding you is just... bullshit, man!" He rubbed his temples with frustration; Pierce's words had a bad habit of never matching his passion.

"They aren't wackos. They're drawing from the same playbook as us. Just being a little more," Benny almost hesitated, "forceful."

"Don't sugarcoat it. Violent," Pierce said with a resurgence of courage, steamrolling the splintering floor with his Birkenstocks, "Violence immediately negates any message we send with peaceful protest. Think Gandhi, Vietnam, Tiananmen Square, Martin Luther King for Christ's sake. We really have a chance to send a powerful message to the greedy capitalists at Wall Street, even if it takes some time, but the instant we add violence to our protest then it's game over for us." Flushed and nearly out of breath he settled back in his lawn chair with a puffed chest, dragging on his cigarette, sending another wisp of smoke into the dense atmosphere. His pride was viscous.

All heads on deck swerved to face Benny, ears raised tall. Nothing would convince the rubberneckers, who each individually expressed their disapproval with their friends' newfound anarchist bent in the days prior, but they were more than content to entertain this piece of political theater.

"Say they sit in for justice," Benny would retort to himself an hour too late, *"sit and stare like conscienceless ants all night."* He still had to respect the fighting spirit of Pierce, perpetually inflating itself into a balloon afloat with righteous hot air. Benny searched for a needle.

He had none. His slack jaw spelled victory for the moderates. David was no help, silent in the chair behind him. Tucked in the corner beneath a technicolor coat of autumn, Benny's reluctant ally kept his lips tight and gaze straight on the leaf in his hand, nearly comatose in thought. He swore he could see the colors drain through the wrinkled veins, out the stem, dissolved as blood red droplets of natural ink into the swirling porch cloud. Both young men were trying to articulate the words Walden had preached only a few days ago.

In the moment, his speeches were insurmountable. Benny could not even call them speeches. Walden used no megaphones or podiums. Body language amplified the gravity of his words better than volume ever could. A belt of pamphlets rattled at his side while he gestured the tenets and goals of his splinter movement, David and Benny eager listeners among a small but captivated flock. First glance would not betray his stance as a rebel outlier among rebel outliers. Benny envisioned a bloody totem of scarlet letters and spiked bands, baggy pants torn with the holes and scars of G8 conferences and labor strikes, a figure of bloody history weighed down with seeping bloodshot eyes that wept tear gas and could swim in pepper spray. Rather, the figure before him hid no scars beneath an unassuming orange tee, "DELANEY SOFTBALL CHAMPIONS '88," nor scars around a positively dorky bowl cut plucked straight from the '96 yearbook.

"Of course," he would say, *"Walden is not my given name. But it is my real name. You must embody the ideals of justice you stand for in totality if you seek to make them real etc etc,"* he would lecture. Benny never actually read Thoreau before September 30th. On

October 4th, he could challenge any scholar on the meat and meaning of "Civil Disobedience." Still, he found a match in Pierce, by far the most fervent Occupier of the friend group. They sparred against each other with the mutual text, like dueling preachers slamming the others' interpretations of the same verses.

"I think this Walden has some right ideas," Benny said with a thumb in Walden's pamphlet, frosted air forming and vanishing around his mouth in the frigid tent, "Occupy is deadlocked. No one knows where to take the protest next. We just stand around and meander and vote like a bunch of idiots. Know what that reminds me of?"—he did not need to say it, but neither Pierce nor David took him very seriously—"this damn hegemonic capitalist society we're protesting against. Says here that 'A minority is powerless when it conforms to the majority,' and that 'it is irresistible when it clogs by its whole weight.' Maybe breaking off into a more driven sub-movement is a good idea. Walden is really onto something."

David rolled his eyes with a curt laugh.

"You're not an anarchist."

Benny started to believe Pierce and David. David started to believe Benny. They both believed Walden when he announced the split was happening.

"Save the date: November thirtieth," he said to the tent crowded with lieutenants, "The two month anniversary, as you know, two months of standing around sending a vague, unfocused message to no one in particular. The common Occupier has told you that this vagueness is a strength, allowing for a generality that woos the majority, the 99%. But this message of vagueness, delivered simply by standing around and arguing, transformed what was once a band of activists for justice into a cloud of uncertainty. Remaining among their ranks would be as useless as panhandling outside Goldman Sachs, or voting in a two-party system where both parties fuck the common man. But our voices will not get lost in the sea of mediocrity. We stand in secrecy, and with few people, but what we lack in numbers we make up for in strength: the strength of action, and the strength of disobedience, and the strength of an idea, for with a good idea one man can conquer the weak wills of a million that stood against him."

If in another situation, spotlighted at the center of his own Shakespearean play or melting in front of a TV camera in front of a stunned studio audience, Walden would have seen his announcement greeted with a thunderous round of applause, cosmic and massive enough to force the walls of government come crashing down, congress scurrying to sign letters of resignation accepting all blame for social and fiscal inequality, the gender wage gap, corporate malevolence, the lies of Enron and Worldcom, Fannie Mae and Freddie Mac, rising tax rates, uneven contracts, and all sixty-eight grievances written up in the last three weeks by the Committee Against Greed, now in its third and penultimate draft. The committee would not need to submit the finalized draft, expected in mid-December provided the Committee For Social Justice finds the terms and demands acceptable, as Walden would find himself crowned the true mayor of Boston, speaker for the people with stolen blackjack and broken brick in hand, sash dropped over his shoulder by two convenient doves, and he would stand before the grand mass of Occupiers, beholden to his wise countenance with misguided divine reverence, to utter the liberating manifesto society had waited one hundred and forty eight years to properly hear:

"*Go forth, free citizens, and live equally!*" would be the simple enunciation that would render Walden obsolete, dissolving under his sash into the fine purple beads of an idea that spread throughout the Greater Boston Area like dandelion seeds, passing the reins of democracy to the basest form of people: *all* people.

No, it would not go like that. If the anarchist agenda had the same ends as the Occupiers, why would the naysayers suddenly sprout ears and fly away? Violence would only aggravate. Of course, this was also within Walden's modus operandi. "*Prison is the natural refuge of the activist and a crutch of the dimwitted,*" he would pontificate shirtless atop a pillar of newspapers and skulls, the sleeves of his shoulders tattooed a deep and bloody green. "*News of our sacrifice will draw enough eyes to pierce through iron bars with their gazes. The revolution will set us free!*" And a final hurrah would echo, the anarchist cavalry charging headfirst with spears against rubber bullets, the silent majority of Occupy expressing their mute disapproval as line by line of mohawked veterans tramples their arms and faces. Each anarchist would be summarily cut down by the steel-hooded centurions of oppression, as expected, as planned. A single crack from a riot shield would send Walden toppling from his golden horse, piles of dust kicked up from the mayhem obscuring his inevitable suicide:

"*The whole world's a prison to contain our cause! Fight to the end! Let no free man escape alive! The end is now!*" Channels two through two hundred would report the tragedy of Walden's Last Stand as it happened, box seats for the occasion graciously purchased by their host a week in advance. Such a regrettable sacrifice, the heart of Occupy will surely take months to recuperate from the damage Mayor Menino in his ivory tower has done, but even so its fiery soul burns brighter than ever with vicarious vigor. Walden's body will not lie a-moulderin' in the grave in vain, and within two weeks Anderson Cooper is calling for a reevaluation of the electoral college, the dissolution of World Bank, and a solid gold plaque commemorating the turning point of civilization made from the teeth and chains of hedge fund managers, their moral prisons slowly descending into a cauldron of boiling silver.

But what is to say that this would work either? Walden only plans on using small riot tactics, sticks and stones but not to break bones. Word around the tent has it that a thuggish upstart nicknamed Engels is thinking about splintering off from the splinter, starting his own revolution powered by guerilla tactics of the urban jungle. What if that is still too tame to get eyes and ears? Guevara would take it from there, fresh-faced sixteen year old straight out of the Junior Prom, but more well-read than ten of your highest ranking modern philosophers. A one-man committee of mass destruction, Engels and Walden combined could not match the bloodshed Guevara is willing to cause for the cause. What was the cause again? Sade could not answer, but the nine-year-old revolutionary could fulfill it lickity-split from his kindergarten outpost, camouflage overalls hiding a tactical genius too precious to associate with the likes of Guevara, Engels, or Walden. And you don't even want to know about Indira. Barely a babe, transmitting coded messages to the revolution via umbilical cord, she bares her teeth in the most radical and uncompromising fashion of them all. Justice will be found by any and all means, each more brutal than the last, each vehemently disowning the proceeding sect with increasing prejudice, each completely justified within the same context, the same quote.

"How is there not a blood shed when the conscience is wounded?" all the demagogues would quote in five-part dissonance before a crowd united by their deep glaring divides, *"Through this wound a man's real manhood and immortality flow out, and he bleeds to an everlasting death. I see this blood flowing now."* Bleeding Boston, muskets bared at the Back Bay, igniting the methane clouds that covered student porches from Worcester to Roxbury. The forces would meddle and battle with each other over the trivialities of social war while the more established military complexes grinned and watched. This would be a situation not too far from Benny's own reality.

Benny stared at the pamphlet, the Thoreau original many Occupier's called a bible, co-opted by Walden with a black-and-white scribbled title page and preface: "CIVIL DISOBEDIENCE: A DISORIENTATION GUIDE TO *REALLY* PROTESTING." No more interpretation. Too dangerous, too fuzzy. Remember Pierce, remember Gandhi, remember Aesop's tortoise. He tore the title page off, dropping to the cold concrete into a pile of desiccated brown leaves.

The anarchists did not smoke. Cigarettes were just another limb of corporate hegemony, a tax you paid in dollars as well as health. Benny needed one badly the day of Walden's splintering. No more meetings in tents: they all stood out in the open, hidden, mingled with their moderate colleagues. Benny felt sick, his throat itched. David was no help; he had turned completely. A coarse brick in his pocket irritated the hairs on his thigh, but a broad grin squelched any pain, hungry with anticipation for the feast of chaos and justice to come.

The revolutionaries slowly congealed into a united force before the glass wall of riot shields and caution tape. Most of the crowd did not know what was going on. If this event were brought up before one of the People's Committees, it surely would have been shot down.

Benny lagged with hesitant steps, but David plowed on, reaching into his pocket for the brick. Enough.

"David! David! David! Enough of this shit, okay? Pierce and Dan and all them were right, this cannot be a good thing. Occupy is a big mess of its own but violence is not a reasonable alternative." David would not pay attention, so Benny tried grabbing his shirt. The anarchist wrested free instantly, a deep red glare soaking through his brown eyes.

"Enough of *your* shit. We tried it the peaceful way. We tried using your big words and rhetoric. Now we need to make a statement."

"You won't start a revolution, man."

"You think I don't know? It wasn't about a revolution. Ever. It's about standing up for what you believe in, and fighting back against the bastards who choke that down with death and greed. You learned nothing from Walden. You're not an anarchist. You're still part of the fucking machine."

The red flush of anger drained instantly from Benny's face, sucked into the atmosphere leaving behind a pallid husk of a shell of a young man. David continued his stride towards the row of staunch civil guards unabated, finger on the stiff red trigger in his pocket. Benny stood silent as a projection, the ideals and whims of the world filling his mind back up breath by breath as he sucked in the great cloud of public protest that hung above him, the taste of smoke and ashes mixing sweetly with the spice of sober discord.

Looking downward, he saw the origin of the smell. In a mound of grey leaf carcasses, at the feet of the young grey Benny himself, lay another brick. Smoke plumed upwards from the brick into his nostrils, from a half-finished cigarette quashed upon the brittle mortar that once held buildings together. Benny reached out his hand.

• • •

Paul A. Reilly *is a bachelor from Tufts University. He likes to write, sometimes. Thank you for reading his story or, at the very least, his brief biography.*

Medicine
by e.a.d. sellors

The doctor pressed around
under my right lung
and made some unintelligible
sounds squinting his eyes
a frown appearing on his brow

finally with his spine straightened
looking down at me
sat there looking up
informed me that the liver's grown
over an inch into the lung

but that it wasn't the end of the world
I just had to stop drinking.

• • •

The Sycamore Tree
by Niall O'Connor

Autumn had come again, and the old man knew it could not be put off any longer. The great Sycamore that had seeded itself unbeknownst to him, over twenty years before, had now greedily taken most of the light from his garden. It had to go.

He had become fond of late, of sitting out in the low autumn sun, and he welcomed the happy memories that the warmth returned to his mind and body. If he didn't move, he could feel no aches and pains. The uninvited tree blighted this warmth, and caused him to move his chair repeatedly, in search of the little patches of sunlight, that managed to make their way through. It had to go, — when he still had the strength. The decision was made.

Under the stairs he found the old bow-saw. The blade was rusted. In the old man's memory he could see the glint of sunlight on steel. He remembered the sweet tune it once made, as the blade sang its way, through the soft flesh of woods, wafting the scent of timber across the garden.

He went down through the long grass, picking his way carefully. The tree waited for him, impassive and unafraid. He looked up at its great canopy of drying and dying leaves, spotted with the ugly Tar Spot fungus he knew he should welcome since it signified the air was clean. But he only felt revulsion, that this tree had dared blight his garden with its presence. In the space of only twenty years, it had grown to over fifty feet tall. In the unlikely event that he would want to embrace the thing, his arms would not have been able to encircle its girth.

Its timber was no good for the fire. In ancient times, he heard it had served to make kitchen utensils; its flesh was said to be sweet and clear, but he was no wood carver, so he would kill it, and only because he hated the cold shade, that now spread over his shrinking world.

Still fit for his age, the old man leaned on his saw for a while, and sized up what had now come to see as his adversary. In his mind, he drew lines down from the uppermost branches, down through the main trunk. Lines that he knew gravity worked through. Lines that would dictate, where the tree would fall. These were signs and judgments you took your time with. A rushed or careless assessment, could bring the tree down where you stood, or worse still, it could be hung; the newly felled tree getting support from a neighbour branch. In this case, no one would be able to predict where, or when, it would finally fall. He examined the nearby trees carefully, and saw that if he were to drop it down hill, he would be clear. The added bonus, he observed with satisfaction, was that the trees uphill were straight and had few lateral branches. These could afford him a refuge, if everything went wrong.

The afternoon wind stirred the drying leaves, and he felt a tinge of sadness at what he was about to do. A tree never takes into account the actions of man. It stands resolutely against winds and seasons, prepares itself for frosts and snows and drought. But there was no planning for the hatchet and the biting blade. This tree would fall like so many before it. The tree would fall out of the necessity of a man, before its time, and not of its own volition.

The old man straightened up and stepped forward, his eye fixed on where the first cut would go. It would be the belly cut; the cut that sloped upwards on the away side of the tree. This was the cut that would lead it to fall where he had chosen it would. He wanted it to fall along the boundary, where it could lie until he was ready, and not across into his neighbour's garden, where it might do damage.

After the first scoring of the bark, he put his two hands to the saw, and with each pass, a spray of timber confetti fell to the ground. Eventually, he removed a wedge, not as deep he would have liked, but it was a start. It was not only the blade, but he himself, that had obviously grown blunted, and rusty with age.

At first, he slept well that night, but through his dreaming, ran a definite concern that he could not leave the tree, now that he had started, and a suspicion that the task was going to weigh more heavily, than he had originally estimated. He prayed that if there was a storm, it might be blown down, but only if it came in the night, when nobody was around, and no one could be hurt, or even killed.

Then he thought of the young fellow, next door. The special child. There was no point in telling him to stay away. He never heeded the old man, when he was shooed out of the garden. He just kept coming back. How do you explain danger to one who is always inquisitive, but can never learn? In his sleep, the old man tossed and turned under the weight of what he had started, and would now have to finish.

He should have left it, or paid someone to come in, and do the job with a chainsaw. But he hadn't waited. He had started. Still confident in the memory of the strength that was once his; he had fooled himself into thinking, that it would be an easily completed task. When he was younger, maybe an hour or two's work.

The morning was already tired when he left his bed, and the old man resolutely went back, to what he hoped would not be another full day's work. He believed all big jobs should be broken down into simple steps, as much from necessity as belief. This was the thought he most often comforted himself with, and he knew that if a man sets his mind to anything, he could do it; no matter how small the man. A grain of sand removed, is the beginning of the end of a beach. Even the stones of the great pyramids had to be put in place, one by one.

With such thoughts he kept his mind occupied, as the drudgery of the task he had started, began to wear him down. He steeled his mind against the pain, and the weakness that had so recently begun to infest his body. He worked slowly and methodically, with thought and guile on his side. There was as much time as was needed, these days, and sometimes even more than he wanted, he thought wryly to himself. With that realisation, he found some added energy, and so he continued throughout the day, feeling for where the blade might bite more easily; trying to find easier ways to drag the aged steel, against the pressing weight of the tree. The evening sun, saw the old man still struggling, and when it got too dark to work, he eventually gave up, and slunk back to the house, under cover of darkness.

It was the third day. The morning sun dragged itself over the hill, to the east of the house, and though he had lain for hours, awaiting its arrival, when it did come, he did not want to get up. Across his chest, and down into his arms, it hurt, and whenever he turned in the bed, an involuntary cry of pain escaped from his tortured body. One night's sleep, would not cure this, he knew. But he had worked through pain before, and it was not new to him. All his life had been a celebration of hard, physical jobs, well done, and pain was just another sign of effort, and deserving of respect. This new pain felt different, however. It was in his joints. They all ached, and the old man realised, that this must be what they called 'growing old'. His age was against him.

He ate his breakfast slowly, taking the time to build his mind, as much as his body, for this new resumption of the battle he was locked into. This tree was something that grew. Organic. He knew that he too was organic, but he in addition, he had mind, and mind was not so easily measured. He made his way to where the tree waited impassively. The thought that it was organic and destructible, gave him little relief.

Carefully, he placed the blade in the gaping white mouth that was the sum of his work so far. He started to saw once more. Stroke after stroke, despite his efforts, was slowed by the willful tree. Every few minutes, he had to withdraw, going to sit on the chair he had placed, just uphill from where he worked. Again and again, he returned. The intervals between the work, and the rest, became longer, until even he began to doubt his own ability, to outlive this beast. In a daze, he worked and rested, rested and worked, trying to fill his mind with thoughts of how men felled great trees with stone axes, so they might have heat and shelter; how small men were sometimes dwarfed by great tasks that they nevertheless managed to complete. Then he thought of his forefathers, and how they had made fields where there was bare stone; raising walls to both shelter and aid their efforts. He retreated once more, to where his tribal and spiritual memories lay, always ready to come to his aid when all else failed. He turned to the will, that allows a man to perform drudgery, while still holding the gossamer thin traces of his imagination.

With every pass of the blade, the tree had to be weaker, and with weakness came danger. The old man worried about turning his back on it, even for a moment. In his youth he had heard stories of trees that had killed, as an answer to their tormenters. He eyed again the twisted lower branch, that grew away from the main trunk, before straightening up to the sky. This was the heaviest of the lower limbs, and now he could see that it might force the trunk to twist on its foot, when it was released, and throw the entire weight uphill, against him. He did not know how heavy a tree might be, but he knew it must be measured in tons, and dead weight was heavier than live. He shuddered in fear at the thought of this tree weighing down on him, and realised that his end could be either quick, or slow, depending on the embrace.

Just then, there was a deep throated echoing wrench from within the tree, and he knew that something had given way. He stepped back quickly, but nothing happened. There was silence. The wind still rustled the drying leaves, and the top most branches still swayed gently. There seemed to be no movement from the main trunk. The old man stepped forward and rested his hand on the warm bark, feeling for the slightest hint of a movement. There was none. He did not understand why it was still standing, and so, he began to suspect that it was now choosing its own time and place. He anxiously examined the tree once more, prodding around the gaping wound. He angrily pushed against it. It ignored him. He leaned forward, still prepared to get away quickly, and placed his ear to the trunk. He could hear nothing. And still he knew something had definitely torn inside.

> ...the old man now felt renewed energy, and attacked the tree once more, with the passion of a small child

It was then he remembered his dream from the night before. In this dream he had discovered that at the heart of every tree there were musical strings. Heart chords that sang; the music that all trees make as they sway with their lover, the wind. He had been sad at this discovery, but had quickly forgotten his sadness it when he woke up to the pain of another day's work. Now he remembered clearly. That is what the sound had been; he had cut one of the heart strings. He was sad now; he had spoilt such beauty . . . and for what? A whimsical wish for more light in his garden. It was not right.

In spite of this shame, or because of it, the old man now felt renewed energy, and attacked the tree once more, with the passion of a small child, kicking out with all his energy. He was sorry, but the injury had already been done. He realised, that only in the felling of this tree, could all his half completed actions be redeemed. He did not sleep well that night.

On the final day, the old man rose early. He was angry, and in pain. He wrested himself from the bed, with a cry of anguish, cradling his swollen wrists to his chest. He hobbled from the bed, to the window at the back of the house, hoping against all hopes, that the tree itself might have lain down in the middle of the night. The grass was covered in hoar frost. The tops of the trees were receiving the first heat of the early sun, and the dried leaves that had been frozen in place, overnight, were now falling silently and relentlessly. It was like a snow fall, but it was not pretty, as a snow falls can be. This was a laying down of death; the end of another growing season. The old man stood, holding his aches and pains close to him, and felt the shawl of sadness, fall seductively about his shoulders. The tree still stood amongst its peers, and it too was shedding leaf. The old man shook his head in frustration, for now he knew he had lost an ally. With the canopy gone, the effect of the wind would be greatly diminished.

He went downstairs stiffly, and made himself a cup of tea. He took three paracetamol. The packet said two, but he needed three. This day would have to be the last he thought. He had spent too much time with this tree, and shared too much. It had seen him at his finest, and at his worst. He had probably shared more with this cantankerous, useless, weed of a tree, over the past three days, than he had shared with anyone else in recent years. Silently, he finished his tea, and gathered up his tools, from where they had been dropped the night before.

The tree waited, and the old man examined it, at first, with a mixture of disgust and envy. He placed the saw once more in the gaping mouth, and tried to cut his way inwards, searching for the remaining tensed cords. Again the tree pressed down on his blade, and most of his effort was spent, in simply drawing it through, and pushing it back, through the narrow space.

His neighbours, best dressed, passed on their way to mass, for it was Sunday. The shook their heads, when they saw the old man and what he was doing, but none interfered for he was well known for his stubbornness.

The morning wore on, and the leaves continued to fall, as the frost was burnt away. Then he noticed the drops of liquid. More and more, were appearing on the bared white flesh, above the main cut. The tree was losing its life's blood. He knew then that he would triumph in the end. The more moisture the tree lost, the weaker it would become.

He reached out his index finger to catch one of the drops, and put it reverently to his lips, and when he tasted of it, he found that it was sweet. The old man drew strength from its sweetness, and came back hungrily for more. He smiled as he realised his strength had begun to grow again, and now he sawed cleverly, first on one side, and then on the other, searching out for the remaining heart strings. He remembered, that the Sycamore was related to the Maple, and he wondered if Maple syrup came the same way.

Both his hands were now swollen and bloody, as the blade had gone to its depth, and his knuckles constantly hit against the scarred rim of the widening cut. He ignored the pain. Suddenly there was aloud crack! He jumped away, from where he was braced against the ditch. He waited. All was quiet. The leaves continued their autumn settling, but everything else around him had changed in that single instant. He rushed to pick up, the discarded head of the hatchet that had broken on him, and wedged it into the gap, on his side of the tree. Then with a stone, that he pulled from the ditch, he pounded on the steel wedge, to drive it as deep as possible.

There was another loud crack, and then a third, and a fourth. He stepped quickly away, and waited out of respect, for what he knew would now inevitably follow. Silently, the tree finally lay down, and the old man's spirit soared, from the weight it lifted from his soul. He saw that it had fallen exactly where he had planned, and he was happy.

Then some tears came, from where he thought he had dried up forever, and he allowed them to course freely down his face without wiping them away. They were bitter and salty, as the tears of all men are, unlike the sweet drops he had tasted from the tree. Now he understood, why it is so.

. . .

Niall O'Connor *is a published poet and blogger, and reads regularly at the Writer's Centre and other popular Dublin venues. O'Connor's poems have been published in The Examiner and most recently in The Stoney Thursday Book, thefirstcut#, A handful of Stones, Carty's Poetry Journal, Madrush, Outburst, Corvus, God's and Monsters, A Blackbird Sings, Blue Max Review and others. He was a featured poet at the inaugural Fermoy Poetry Festival 2012. He was also featured in Connotation Press earlier this year.*

Reunion
by Gary Clifton

Bill had been a star athlete for the Hooterville Whupkats, graduating in the mid fifties. Hooterville was a small, dull, Midwestern community known for nothing. Bill's career in sales had carried him far and wide. Hooterville gradually drifted off his radar.

Then, the alumni association tracked him down in retirement at his estate on a private lake in Arkansas. "You don't come, the world ends", they pleaded. Old good natured Bill packed up his wife and made the six hour drive to Hooterville.

On the big night, Bill learned that the reunion was not restricted to his class, but was an alumni gathering of everyone who'd ever attended Hooterville High. He stood in a line of dreary, white haired, many-on-wheels old folks, wondering who the hell they were.

The harried lady volunteer checking off admissions was locked into a frustrating argument about photos on the tables with a tall lady whose face was contorted into a permanent scowl-clone of Bride of Frankenstein. Bill, his knees aching, idly wondered how they would have anyone's photo to put on a table to begin with. It was about the time of evening, back in Arkansas, he'd push his bass boat into action for his regular daily duty of fish population control

By the time Bill and his wife got inside, the head lady in charge was already on the podium, droning on about something neither Bill, nor most of the aged audience could hear, even with their aides turned to max. He did catch a fragment about the regular DJ being a no-show, but a substitute was enroute. The announcement drew a smattering of applause from the sea of ancients attending, mostly white haired ladies twenty years older than Bill. The grim, statistics-monster had already thinned the male crowd.

As the podium lady droned on, the door sprang open. A plump, fleshy man in his mid thirties, bathed in sweat, plunged into the room, pushing a gurney of speakers and electronic gear. Frantically, he began throwing equipment into working order.

The perspiring man stepped behind the podium, arranged some gear, and tossed an electrical around front toward a large speaker. He hurried around the droning lady and collapsed on the floor on his back, hands outstretched in the standard crucifix position. Bill looked around. The podium lady continued, several old folks craned necks to better see the fallen man, but not a soul went to the man's aid.

Concluding that when old folks get together, somebody died all the damned time and nobody got particularly ramped up, he strolled over and knelt to examine the prostrate man. Dilated eyes, no pulse, no spasmodic reaction told Bill the man was deader than last year's Christmas turkey. Nonetheless, definitely no doctor, Bill began chest massage/CPR as vigorously as 74 years of sin and degeneracy allowed.

Quickly approaching exhaustion, he looked around the room and was not really surprised the program was grinding on and no one had come to help. A hotel employee tapped his shoulder. Incredibly the man said: "What are you doing."

"Sort of hoping this poor dead man will sit up and tell me to stop," Bill replied breathlessly. "Does the hotel have a defibrillator."

"Huh?" the man replied.

"Shh," the podium lady said.

EMT's and cops began arriving in blocks of four and gave the victim the works. Bill stood and considered suggesting they move the dead guy aside and turn up the radio at music time, but thought better of it. Who, in a crowd of octogenarians would volunteer in any way to tinker with the music portion of the evening just after a man half their age had cratered doing the job.

The same hotel employee walked back up and said he'd called the D.J.'s home to report the bread winner had just bellied up. Lost in the "shhh's" of the podium lady was that the guy on the floor was not the original. Two pudgy ladies rushed in, tearfully screeching they been told their husband and father, respectively had just died.

"Holy hell," the older of the two screamed. "This lard ass ain't my husband." Both ladies promptly keeled over in separate heaps near the first victim. Even the Podium lady gave up at this point, and with a throwing up of hands, walked off the stage.

EMT's clasped oxygen masks on the two fallen, non-victims. They both quickly recovered and were ushered out of the hotel forthwith - the management apparently anxious to avoid any more victims expiring on the premises than necessary.

The program curtailed, the two pudgy ladies evacuated, the EMT's gathered and with tremendous group effort, heaved the obese DJ onto a gurney. They exchanged knowing, professional glances - the man was gone.

As they wheeled him past Bill holding open the door, the dead man snapped to a sitting position, looked Bill straight in the eye and said: "I gotta a gig to do and you broke by collar bone you idiot." Bill, convinced he was somewhere between the twilight zone and Hell, grabbed his wife and lit a shuck for Arkansas.

Just before he reached the safety of his front door shortly before dawn, an acquaintance, back in Hooterville, called his cellular. The night had not ended when Bill bailed out. The fat guy had survived and was expected to recover. Bill had contributed to saving his life.

However, the original D.J. had been down the road getting some strange, but had told his wife - the fat lady who'd appeared at the reunion - he was at that reunion. When he arrived home at 2:00 A.M. drunk as a fruit orchard boar, he casually told his wife he'd been forced by old folks at the reunion to accept many free drinks. The distraught wife promptly shot him four times. The funeral was scheduled for the following Tuesday.

Bill figured if he lived another day, he'd probably go fishing.

• • •

Gary Clifton, *forty years a cop has about sixty short fiction pieces published or pending with online sites. Clifton has been shot at, shot, stabbed, sued, lied to, frequently misunderstood and is now retired to a dusty north Texas ranch where he doesn't care if school keeps or not. He has an M.S. from Abilene Christian University.*

The Loneliness
by Patrick Jamieson

He watched her lie through tiles of
pane glass,

Obscured, shattered, at last
he drew his own.

She lay submissive in the snow,
like yesterday,

Just like tomorrow, crafting angels
made of bone.

• • •

Patrick Jamieson *is a fledgling writer from Edinburgh, Scotland. Raised into the literary world by his father he held inherent affection for the arts and rejected structured education entirely, choosing instead to learn independently. He has since worked odd jobs to support his artistic ambitions and today somewhat ironically, works for the City of Edinburgh Council in the Adult Education department.*

Thoroughly Modern
by Kirsten Mullen

Six and a half
steps down
second hand white church shoes
prance down the bus's steps
a worn briefcase
stuffed with simple
farm clothes
mud caked laces
from handed down boots
hang out of her father's
physician's bag
turned new world
survival kit.

Pulling her coat tighter
her mother's only
Sears purchase
she turns as the bus
pulls away
her oversized hat
which she believed was
the epitome of fashion
fluttered slightly
a dark suited man
rushes past her
oblivious of her confusion
with one arm stretched to touch his
she let go of her hat
she felt it swept off of her head
in one smooth motion
startled
surprised
gasping she spun on her heel
and slipped.

A pleasant child bends
down
her face lights up
the hand pass hers
and instead steals her
glass slipper
she turns on her side to grab it
back
a young woman
with dark unkempt hair
limps past
slyly she reaches down
and keeps walking
her first accessory
pulling her self up
pushing up off of the
fire hydrant
blowing her side swept bangs
out of her pale face
she straightened her best dress
standing tall
one leg bent
where a shoe should have
been strapped
she looked up
smiling

this was it
all her life's savings
and suddenly
she wanted it more
than when she left
her poor life
because it was in her reach
a dream suddenly a reality
through modern loves.

. . .

Kirsten Lorraine Mullen *is young poet and fictional writer entering her junior year at Moorestown Friends School, a small Quaker high school. She is the secretary of her high school's poetry club and has been published several times in its literary magazine, 'Images'.*

Moving Out After the Divorce
by Stephanie Bradbury

How many times have I climbed these stairs-

The top never too far from the bottom
Only greater expectations

More of a distance to fall

Arms ache with memories of heavy bags
And new babies as I stand here

Surveying the emptiness of fleshless rooms
Showing off their space

And the windows with their lidless eyes
Look to the corners, to the floor, to the sky

As I hold the banister one last time-
A support that never failed

Bare fingers tracing its hopeful shine

That will be gone by noon.

. . .

Stephanie Bradbury *lives in Acworth Geogia with her husband, Brian, and their two children. She loves poetry and started writing as a child. Currently she is working on a B.A. in Creative Writing and works as an emergency room nurse. Her work has recently appeared in Mad Swirl, TurtleWay Journal, and Curio Poetry.*

Two-Ton Paperweight
by Pat Malone

The party had rendered Jake Roberts inebriate and reeking of vomit. He was lying face down in a dumpster, attempting to determine whether or not he was too drunk to escape its walls. After remaining motionless for a few moments, he decided he should focus his energy on locating an exit. A few seconds of wild flailing confirmed his prior notion that such a task was nearly impossible under the thick haze of intoxication, so he groped for his pocket, produced a pack of cigarettes, lit one, and rolled over to face the stars.

Jake had been abandoned in a dumpster at his own social gathering. However, his reason for being dumped in such an unsavory location was perfectly reasonable. He had struck someone at the party across the face in a fit of drunken rage (something about them changing the presets on his Ferrari's radio during a joy ride) and, after receiving a few blows himself, was subsequently transported to the dumpster by two larger gentlemen.

The din of the party was now barely audible in the distance. The gathering had been financed, like everything else in Jake's life, by his late uncle, Big Jimbo. Most of his extended family loathed Jake (and this fact was corroborated by the falling chandelier which nearly killed him during the reading of Big Jimbo's will), but Big Jimbo, adored by the family solely for his money and power, seemed to see something in the man. "Jack," Big Jimbo would always say after smoking his sixth pack of the day, "Don't let these jok'as get to ya. People ain't good f'a nothin'. They'll hold ya back. I'll tell ya, they wouldn't know greatness if they were sodomized by it." Then he'd purchase Jake a new car or hand him a check for a hefty sum of cash.

The only other person in the world who seemed to have a soft spot for Jake was a lover of his by the name of Anabella. A rumor had circulated for quite some time in the Roberts family that Jake was planning to marry her. The story was told in a variety of manners, sometimes involving submarines or Jake ingesting hallucinogenic mushrooms, but the constants were always someone overhearing Jake reading aloud the words he formed on his computer while composing a letter illustrating his romantic intentions.

But Jake's life changed when, contrary to what the surgeon general had predicted, Big Jimbo met his maker at the hands of a cocaine junkie in a Wal-Mart parking lot. Even in death he was able to spoil Jake, and accordingly left him his Malibu beach house and the entire fortune he had obtained from his invention of the spearmint flavored toothpick.

Directly following his acquisition of the enormous fortune, Jake decided to celebrate with a scorpion bowl at the local Chinese restaurant. After an evening of discussing with the restaurant's manager how his year's animal, the snake, on the menu's Zodiac chart didn't reflect his personality in the slightest, he struck Anabella, under the pretense that she was attempting to waste his "hard earned money" after she found a staple in her rice. A lengthy court hearing followed. Jake was sentenced to six months of anger management classes with a pencil-necked kindergarten teacher who explained several times, in great detail, the psychological benefits of taking an hour out of one's day to pet an invisible cat by the name of the Rum Tum Tugger. Anabella, despite expressing even to Jake that she wanted to forgive him, decided to abandon her Bluebeard of a boyfriend after conferring with her mother, a ninety-year old Californian with an affinity for "medical" marijuana who would address Jake using only eloquently composed strings of four-letter profanities.

This event took a significant toll on his mental health, and he retreated into the security of his new Malibu manor. Once Jake finished his six month sentence in "Invisible Cat Stroking 101," the only people who laid eyes on the reclusive billionaire for three years were deliverymen. He passed the time by stomaching expensive wine as though it was Kool-Aid. But his mother, determined that Jake find some acquaintances, decided to plan a party at the mansion behind his back. And where was he now? Lying bacchanalian in a dumpster, soon to be tried once more for assault.

Jake lit another cigarette after his first one had burned out. Shackled by his own intoxication, he decided his only option was to wait until morning, and briefly chuckled at the idea of someone with his amount of wealth spending the night in a dumpster. After a few more drags on his cigarette, he fell asleep with the smoldering butt in his mouth.

It was about six in the morning when the waste receptacle erupted in a violent series of tremors. Confused as to what was going on, Jake forced himself to his hands and knees and stumbled, half asleep and completely hungover, across the dumpster. Before Jake could reach the edge, the dumpster abruptly tipped. A sudden landslide of waste products caused the garbage, which he had spent the night sleeping on top of, to end up covering him entirely. A few faint lines of sunlight danced through spaces in the waste, but the area was soon plunged into darkness by the sudden slamming of a door. Somewhere behind him, an engine roared to life and the vessel was set in motion. He attempted to cry out, only to have a viscous fluid trickle into his mouth and set him gagging. The fear of this occurring again kept him quiet for the rest of the ride, even with the garbage truck's door opening and closing repeatedly.

After about thirty minutes, Jake found himself caught in another stampede of filth and approximately five feet deep in a pile of trash. The muffled staccato of heavy machinery could be heard somewhere nearby, so Jake's assumption was that he had been deposited at the city dump. He didn't scream, figuring that in his mid-twenties he was perfectly able of climbing out from under a few feet of garbage. When the truck's engine faded off into the distance and Jake could be certain there was no danger of it backing over him, he began to wriggle about. The initial struggle proved to be quite tiresome, and he became aware that he had severely underestimated the difficulty of climbing out from under two-hundred pounds of trash.

When his stamina had been replenished by a momentary period of rest, Jake began to fight again, using dense objects which lay nearby to drag himself through the sea of waste. He had progressed about a foot when a sharp sensation traveled through his hungover head due to the loud sound of some sort of machine engaging thirty feet above his head. He winced, swore, and clamped down his forefinger and thumb on the bridge of his nose. Of course, a headache proved to be the least of his problems when a mangled, two ton chunk of metal came crashing through the garbage above him. He screamed, forgetting the reason he had remained quiet the entire truck ride, and gagged again as his mouth filled with a substance he now recognized as a milkshake which had been sitting in a freezer for two years. A collection of symbols came within a foot of his face, and an immense amount of weight was added to his gut. Had he been able to, he would have curled up into a ball and braced himself for the embrace of death. But he found himself wholly incapable of movement, and began to thrash his head like Joe Bonham when he came to conclusion that the collision had paralyzed him from the neck down. However, this idea was soon refuted by movement in his various digits and appendages.

The balmy realization that Jake was neither paralyzed nor dead, but merely trapped, flowed over him. His panic subsided and his exceedingly tense muscles relaxed. Under this condition, he was able to focus his attention on the varied assortment of symbols which he had come face to face with. Judging by the font of the symbols and the material upon which they were printed, they were apparently the text of a license plate. He decided, after considering the amount of effort it would take to turn his head, that he had no option but to read what he now recognized as letter and numbers. At that point he quite nearly had an aneurysm. He was looking at the shredded remains of his Ferrari. He determined that some drunken idiot at the party had crashed it, and plans were conceived to extract revenge upon the vandal.

Jake began to squirm again, but immediately stopped moving once he realized that the Ferrari had forced itself down, down even harder on his body. Evidently, with each disturbance in the garbage pile Jake created, the car's weight would come down on him significantly harder. He screamed, but the sound was drowned out by the machinery. A mental battle against the instinct to move began. The warrior remained as still as possible in his frenzied state, now wildly pivoting his head and feeling around for something that could help him. When his search returned no results, he fell still.

Here was Jake Roberts, the world's youngest billionaire, about to die under his own Ferrari in the city dump. He just laid there for a bit, taking shallow breaths and attempting to devise a plan to escape. More than anything, he craved a drink. Squirming a bit more, he attempted to reach for the pocket which contained his flask, only to feel the weight of the car pressing down harder. He gave up on satisfying his urge, and began to grope, more carefully this time, in the dim light for something, anything, that could potentially save his life. He found destroyed speakers, shattered flat-screen televisions, shredded leather furniture, and various other formerly expensive items which someone in Malibu had once prized. He discovered a leather ottoman which was approximately his own size and shape, about two feet from him. He frantically yanked on the only object which could potentially save his life and, realizing that dragging something his own mass through a dense blob of waste would be a nearly impossible undertaking, released it and fell still.

Jake stared at the unreachable ottoman for a few moments and glimpsed a grotesque little louse squirming in one of the leather's many tears. The fact which he had been denying for so long finally wormed its way into his mind: nothing here could help him. He was doomed to die. It was almost funny; the fate which he had fought in the frenzied fashion of an animal caught in a trap seemed almost soothing when there was nothing left to do but face it. The artificial heartbeat of the dump's clanging machinery had become an almost pacifying din. The chunk of metal which he had prized so much at one time had never looked so beautiful. He felt safe under it. Nobody could hurt him under his Ferrari.

Then, in what Jake had assumed to be isolation, a voice rang out. "Well, well, if it ain' ol' Jack." Jake caught of whiff of alcohol and burning tobacco to his left and pivoted his head in that direction. And there, completely tangible, lay all three-hundred pounds of chain-smoking, binge drinking Big Jimbo. Unable to speak, Jake weakly nodded at his uncle. "Ya know Jack, I'm proud a' ya. Don't let the rest a' these jokers get to ya. People ain't good f'a nothin'. They'll hold ya back."

Jake found himself in agreement with Big Jimbo's glorious teachings. It was almost funny, Jake thought, how both him and his beloved uncle would meet their maker under the wheels of a car. But the similarities between their deaths would not end there. The potent image of Big Jimbo's wake, empty save for Jake and an extremely pretentious undertaker, slithered onto the silver screen of his mind's eye. And the screen erupted in flames, scorched away to reveal the horrible truth that had been hidden behind it: Jake would die alone. Once more Jake groped wildly for his flask, and screamed at the top of his lungs when he couldn't reach it. Horrible revelations swarmed into his mind. He had spent his life alone. He recalled the way his nerves had screamed for the touch of another human during his three year period of isolation, only to have their protests drowned away with expensive Merlot. He had watched the wasted years wither and rot away as he cut himself off from human contact. So then and there, Jake, sober as he had ever been, decided that he would not die alone under a two-ton paperweight. He felt an immense power bubble up from deep within him, and erupt from his lips with a primal cry of, "Anabella!"

So he began to flail and crawl and scream with no fear of milkshake dripping into his mouth. He wriggled as the car's weight began to increase on his abdomen. He could feel the individual fibers of every muscle screaming out as they struggled towards the light. He fought with the heroism of Giles Corey under the enormous mass which threatened to push him into death at any moment. He decided that if he ever got out of the garbage, he would keep fighting. He would fight Anabella's stoned mother and he would fight, with every muscle fiber in his body, for Anabella. He would go home and take a sledgehammer to his TV and all of his worldly possessions. He would torch his house with Molotovs made from all his expensive liquors and laugh as it burned to the ground. He began to push himself backwards under the car, and found that the weight on his stomach was partially relieved. So he pushed deeper and deeper into the garbage, until he noted that the car had become caught in the trash and there was an inch of space between him and it. He drew upon the last of his strength, and forced himself from the decaying pile of waste and worms into the outside world. He emerged from the garbage like a snake slithering from its old skin, triumphant, and leaped to his feet. Basking in the sun, he cried out to the and began to stagger towards several dump workers who had come to investigate what they took to be a mental patient playing William Wallace in the garbage. Jake threw his arms around the first worker who reached him in a tight embrace, and broke down sobbing.

    The homely garbage man uttered something entirely incomprehensible, to which Jake replied, "Thank you, oh God, thank you." A soft breeze blew from the West, and Jake felt a slight chill over his slime and ash coated skin. "Lordy," said the garbage man, "We've got to get you washed off." But his words were lost. Jake was a million miles away from the dump. As the moist tears slithered down his cheek, he gazed off at the sun peaking over the horizon. It had never looked so beautiful.

. . .

Stop Holding On
by M.N. O'Brien

Intertwined through the rails of the cruise
ship, the lovers chose
not to abandon
the safely docked vessel...
Hey! It would be much too lonely without us.

We weren't there to demonstrate against
safety procedures, or even see
the strength for ourselves or compete
as couples do. No one believed
she loved to be vulnerable to the wind.

Something can be said
about our pant legs that rippled
in the breeze, our sleeves that were pinned
between our arms and the rail,
and as the captain claimed, our sanity.

I thought a bystander imagined us falling
from the flashes of cameras.
He tried to get them
to stop, but fell himself off the dock,
in the water, and laughed when he surfaced.

We untangled
ourselves and joined him
in laughter. Then we jumped in,
then the crowd and the captain.
First bodies, then laughter, filled the air.

. . .

M.N. O'Brien *received his B.A. from Roanoke College, where his work was published in On Concept's Edge and received the Charles C. Wise Poetry Award. He was most recently published in SOFTBLOW, The Camel Saloon, and Counterexample Poetics. He currently lives somewhere in the Smoky Mountains and despises writing about himself in the third person.*

Of Higgs and Flame
by Matthew Sissom

Every Friday and Saturday night the Quick Chick's parking lot would fill with the signature rides of Rowan Randolph High's designated elite. Styrofoam cups and expired blunts would litter the lot on Sundays and flutter to collect along the town's main drag. This Sunday, Darren Schuldt staggered away from his mother's minivan, the soles of his Converse All-Stars dragging through the viscous sludge that had pooled around the edges of the wheelchair ramp—the byproduct of a Quick Chick Saturday night gathering. Darren speculated which trace elements were present: regurgitated potato wedges, Sour Apple Pucker residue, and a half-and-half semen/urine adhesive.

"Darren," his mother coughed, "I gotta be at bingo before six so I can get my fifteen dollars from your aunt Shirley. Place is gonna be a madhouse, so I gotta have time to drop you off and get there before they open."

Darren paused and swiveled on a high-top axis to meet his mother's glare. Her face was its own form of kitsch art. Darren's eyes were recalibrating—having suffered from the previous night's gravity bong exposure—and were attempting to make sense of the shit images piercing his retinas.

"I don't get off work until a quarter till six."

"Well, I don't know what to tell you, Dare." His mother shifted the van into gear, her turquoise fingernails clacking against the Cheshire Cat custom gearshift knob. "I've gotta be there by six." She leaned forward to reach for the ashtray, her Malt-O-Meal underarm flaps wagging to expose a moist nest of deodorant cakes.

"Goddamnit. Fine, I'll try to find another way home. All right?"

"Later hun."

Darren watched her drive toward the exit and swerve to narrowly miss the green Dodge Neon that was pulling in. Darren's mom, completely at fault, honked and cursed out of the window. Darren watched Kandi pull into her normal spot with his shoulders poorly postured, and his feet now firmly attached to the asphalt. His hands began to sweat as he removed his Quick Chick cap to wipe his brow. Kandi opened her door and emerged from the Marlboro Light cloud that had failed to fully escape from the crack of her window on the ride in. Darren watched as she pulled her hair through the eye of a ponytail scrunchie. Her glitter eyeshadow reacted like moondust under the flares of light creeping over the roof of the neighboring motel.

"Who the shit was that?" Her eyes shifted to Darren. She flicked the last cigarette out of her soft pack and tossed the preceding butt into a breeze that carried her trailer park aroma toward Darren.

"Just some lady asking what time we open," Darren answered.

Kandi sparked her lighter and arched her back into a stretch. Darren's eyes traced her outline—she was definitely his brand. Her body, slightly obscured by her Quick Chick uniform, seemed to be all right. Her breasts were accentuated by the purse strap tugging on the material between them. The cherry on the end of her cigarette flickered as she seductively weezed an additive stream into the quiver of her lungs. Kandi coughed and convulsed just enough to expose her belly button ring to Darren's violating eyes. The fucker sparked—It sparked!—and shot back under its tee-shirt-sheath. She slid on her Quick Chick cap and looked toward him.

"You stoned or something?" she asked.

"What? No. I had a long night."

"Really?" She took a few steps toward him, and, for a second, Darren was positive she gave him her I'd-fuck-you-eyes. She breathed her scent into his neck from a few feet away. "Do anything crazy?" Darren held strong against a tremble.

"I, well—not really—we just," Darren cut his voice off at the sound of the IROC-Z barreling into the parking lot. His body started to jellify next to Kandi, but for a less desirable reason. Kandi rolled her eyes and began walking toward the diner's employee entrance. The driver pulled in front of her to block her progress and opened his door.

"What the hell do you want, Ethan?" Kandi shouted.

Ethan lowered his sunglasses just enough to expose the reds of his eyes. "Baby, you still pissed about yesterday? I told you to fucking drop it."

"Well, I can't just drop it." Kandi's hand skimmed over her right eye socket. Darren noticed her makeup was thicker on that side.

Ethan's gaze shifted to Darren. The sounds of dubstep blared from the IROC-Z's customized sound system and slid out the door, humming their fuckass song against the excretions that held Darren firmly in place. Ethan pointed at him.

"Go inside, Dognuts."

Darren became an ancient dragon, raining fire and fury on Ethan. He reveled in the rage and picked the flesh from Ethan's tug-and-fuck face with his freshly born fangs.

The fantasy was short-lived.

"Get. The fuck. Inside. Space Jam." Ethan's mouth curled into a sneer as the nickname hit its mark. Darren was thrust back into the seventh grade. Gym class. Ethan and the other oversized flunkies were shoving him into a locker in the girls' dressing room—the only scraps of clothing he had on were his Space Jam underwear.

Kandi looked at him with an apologetic expression. Darren snapped at her.

"I'm going to count the registers, be inside in five minutes."

His world may not have included trailer park trophies like Kandi, but it did come with a job in fast food management. Albeit a part-time, non-salary gig, his power at Quick Chick was nearly absolute.

The grease-crusted portrait of the owner, Artie Wineville, bore down on Darren as he passed it to unlock the registers behind the counter. The night manager, Benny, forgot to wipe down the windows before he closed the night before. Spit streaks remained frozen in time on the outside—grease stains and fingerprints fudged the inside. Belched vapors of word vomit crawled through Darren's nose hairs, his lips still and mute. Darren's dragon form returned and ran a charred talon through Benny's anus. His eyes were lit like the bowels of the mountain that spawned him, and he watched as Benny's body slid across the parking lot alongside the shrieks and screams of the teens loitering near the drive-thru.

Ethan had Kandi by the arm. She was almost crying now. Darren would have felt sorry for her, but Ethan wasn't worth interfering with. Kandi managed to free her arm long enough to make it to the employee entrance. Ethan followed her path through the murky glass and issued what could only be perceived as some type of warning glance to Darren before slinking down in the seat of his whip. The dubstep volume level that followed rippled across the un-emptied mop bucket under the drive-thru window. Ethan managed to hold his stare, his sun-glassed eyes while driving, long enough to meet Darren's eyes through the glass perimeter of the restaurant.

"I hate him," Kandi squelched. "He hit me you know."

Darren hip-checked the register drawer into a ding. "I'm gonna cut and bread some chicken. Take the front?" Kandi nodded and wiped her smearing raccoon eyes. The kitchen was Darren's favorite place to work. He loved the sound of gristle snapping with each downward thrust of his cleaver—garbled flesh tearing, organized into edible clumps. His fist would grow discolored from chicken matter, but he refused to wipe it off.

Darren buried his world in the chicken he cooked. All of his pain and disappointment lived in the breaded chunks and were cooked away—part of the chemical change that occurred when the meat was dunked into a 375-degree grease-bath. His mother's adventures in un-employment, his father's permanent vacation to Canada—served alongside gravy-drenched mashed potatoes. Darren would stare into the horror of the oil and absorb himself in its wrath. The snapping hiss would linger in his dreams. Dreams that, like the dragon, remained locked away and personal—waiting for the universe to set them loose.

"Darren, do you know anything about this coupon?" Kandi stood at the register with an old woman whose iron jaw hovered stiff and relentless above the counter of Quick Chick on nearly every Sunday for the past quarter century.

"Hello, Mrs. Harrison. What can I do for you?"

"You can train your employees to run these coupons from the Sunday paper—"

Her voice trailed off into the part of Darren's mind that acted like a gizzard for bullshit. He issued some responses and cordial exchanges, but these were simply rocks grinding the seed of her voice into an easily digestible mush. Darren satisfied Mrs. Harrison's demands and she walked away contented and full of chicken.

This was how Sunday passed. Darren breathed fire in depths of the kitchen while Kandi executed a holding pattern near the front counter. Kandi barely spoke to Darren, and, when she approached him, Darren would find a way to brush her off. This was the indifferent existence he preferred.

But it was closing time, and Ethan returned. Darren was making a batch of chicken to split with Kandi, when the sounds of dubstep again fucked the stomach of his brain. The jelly feeling returned to the sub-waist area of Darren's body. Kandi looked defeated as she finished wiping the counters. Ethan walked inside.

"Kandi, let's go. I wanna take you somewhere to eat where Space Jam hasn't jacked off in the ranch." Ethan moved toward the counter, his eyes bloodshot as uppers and downers fought for control of his body. Kandi turned to Darren.

"Go ahead, Kandi. See you tomorrow."

Kandi grabbed her purse from the employee closet and made her way around the counter. Ethan slapped her ass, and Kandi pushed him away.

> Darren buried his world in the chicken he cooked.

"Cut it out. Don't fucking touch me. I'll talk to you, but you can't touch me right now."

"Don't be a bitch about it. I said I didn't mean it. You shouldn't have let me drink before the party. You know how I get. I need you, babe." Ethan clutched Kandi's ass and ran his nose down her neck.

"Goddamnit, Ethan! Stop!" Kandi slapped the sunglasses from his face. Ethan's hand came down on Kandi's face three times in two seconds. She crumpled to floor.

Darren had once read an article online that discussed the smallest fraction of time physicist's studied at the Large Hadron Collider in Switzerland. The exact science was too complex and the subject too foreign-place for Darren to fully understand all of the equations and multi-theory analyses, but he understood that time and matter are connected through an infinite number of sub-levels. Multiple factors are processed and thrust by Higgs Boson particles, x-forces, brown dwarfs, and other shit Darren could never possibly understand, into the existence of decision.

One small fraction of any micro-sample of time pivots on shit Darren could never see or illustrate to another human being without a bevy of flow charts and pocket-protector-clinging virgins from MIT. Forces that now pushed and shoved the universe to the tip of Darren's tongue and issued forth a glimpse into the expanding unknown.

"Stop it, Motherfucker."

It took everyone a moment to realize the voice had come from Darren. Ethan stilled his hand. Kandi's weeps were cresting between five-second lung gasps. Ethan took two strides toward the counter.

"What the fuck? Did you bust a circuit? Did you just—"

"I said stop hitting her. Get the fuck out of my restaurant." Darren wiggled his wrist in order to draw Ethan's gaze. He was clutching a bubbling batch of grease-drenched chicken—the oil residue of which bled the fiery songs of Mercury.

"You realize what you're doing right now, Space Jam? I'm going to fucking kill you." Ethan kept talking. Eyes of a sleeping beast flickered somewhere just behind Darren's pupils. "I am going to fucking destroy you,

Space Jam. Come out from behind that counter and we'll—"

Darren leapt over the counter, and Ethan was beneath the full spread of the dragon's wings as chicken and scalding grease were rained upon him. His flesh was a splitting hotdog. Ethan tried to brace himself with his arms, but the dragon kept drenching him in the infernal screams of an ancient rage. Fire and flame left Ethan wrenching toward the door, crawling toward the rotting lot that spawned him, his flesh smearing the floor with blood and chunks of skin-infused chicken matter. Kandi, shocked and battered, ran to take cover behind Darren. She was no longer crying, and the dragon retreated to the ancient fires of his home.

Darren felt her grasp and determined that it was good. Her eyes were moist, and spittle had gathered at the corners of her mouth. Darren flipped the switch on the cooling fans perched near the fryers behind them. His hand ran along the outlines of her battered face and up to remove the cap and scrunchie from her head. Kandi's hair, oiled from the day, struggled to flow in the freedom of the breeze they now shared.

"Darren, what do we do when he comes back?"

Somewhere, on one of those subatomic levels, the dragon lie in waiting—waiting for the universe to push it forth, to spin it into a frenzy, and to cool it in the bathing winds of triumph. Kandi's eyes were drying, and her normal color was beginning to seep through newly-formed bruises. Darren smiled sympathetically.

"Give me a ride home?" Kandi nodded as Darren's hand moved up her back to meet the cradle of her neck.

Darren kissed Kandi, and the taste of her tobacco afterlung would haunt his mouth for an age.

. . .

Matthew Sissom *is a Graduate Assistant at Southeast Missouri State University currently teaching freshmen-level writing. His poetry has been published recently in the lit mag Constellations. He trudges through life alongside the Mississippi River—watching baseball, playing video games, and reading upcoming fictioneers. He expects to be thrust into fatherhood sometime during the winter of 2012 following the birth of his son.*

Protest
by Annemarie Ni Churreain

One cut and the hair worn since childhood
fell upon the floor
dead soft.

A spear-thistle;
her new, bald skull
refused order.

She belonged to heather
and in tail-streams
cupping frogs,

delighting
in the small, green pulse of life
between palms,

not here:
at the dark centre of reunions, separations,
starved of air.

This was a protest of love, against love
demanding
sun, rain, wilderness.

From a finger, she slid a band
placed it underfoot,
pressed down

until the stone
made the sound of a gold chestnut
cracking open.

. . .

Thermonuclear Daydreams

by Douglas Sterling

I've been dreaming about thermonuclear war again. Daydreaming also. If I suffer the slightest indignation, if the waiter gets my order wrong, if I miss a belt loop on my pants--my first reaction is to fantasize about mushroom clouds on the horizon.

I guess I'm turning into my father.

The last time I visited Dad he told me that he hoped we'd all get nuked. He said it would be nice to see the world end before he bought the farm. He said, "That way I won't feel like I missed out on nothin'."

My father's apocalyptic daydreams started right after he retired. One day he was in his La-Z-Boy, watching Dialing For Dollars, guzzling scotch, and the Emergency Broadcast Signal started up. He scooted from the cushion cover with an indignant honk and came stumbling down the hall.

"World's ending."

I didn't bother looking up. I was busy playing Atari.

"Hey. Hermann. Did you hear what I said? In a few minutes," he says, "A firestorm will sweep across the land destroying all the shopping malls. There won't be any more video games, any more Michael Jacksons, any more Bubble Yum. Gone, gone, gone."

He went back to the living room, turned the sound on the television all the way up, and came back down the hall like a boomerang.

"Do you hear that? That's the greatest thing I've ever heard. Hooray! My new favorite song. Next comes the flash. You'll be able to see straight through your hands-- you'll see the veins squirming around, your eyeballs will melt, and you'll go up like a torch. Woosh!"

"I don't have time for this," I said. "I'm playing Missile Command."

He kicked the Atari to the floor, climbed up on the footstool, and spread his arms like the Cristo Redentor. I could hear the voice saying it was only a test, but my father was in a rapturous state. He was elated.

"I didn't miss a thing, Harriet!" He stared through the ceiling, vindictively addressing my mother in heaven. "I've outlasted history! Take that, Hitler! You fell asleep before the end of the movie! Alexander the Great, Napoleon, Teddy Roosevelt! Hah! You all missed the punch line! I won! Grover Grabby is the last man left standing!"

At this point the Emergency Broadcast Signal stopped and Bob McLean's voice came rumbling down the hall, announcing a winner. My father's arms flopped to his sides, he disembarked the footstool, and trudged back on down the hall mumbling to himself.

Strange as it may seem, I'm jealous of my father's catharsis. I can't tell anyone about my dreams--day, night or otherwise. If anyone knew, they might say I'm suffering from exhaustion, they might strip me of my dignity, accuse me of psychopathy or treason--they might tell me I'm no longer fit to be President, which is why I've kept my dreams to myself.

So here I am at my desk. I've pulled the bottle of Macallan from its hiding place, the telephone has danced into my hand, and I'm on the line with the Russkies. I can't hold back. I tell them my apocalyptic secret. They tell me I'm drunk. I say, I used to be the quarterback for the Harrison Hawks and guess what suckers I still have the football. There's an awkward pause and then I explain that I'm referring to the nuclear football, the one that has all the launch codes. They curse at me and I let out a drunken presidential snigger. They tell me I'm a powerless figurehead. I blurt out sensitive information, things their allies shared in secret; I tell them about traitors within their ranks, breaches, leaks.

The next morning the shrill ring of the phone throttles me awake.

"White House. President speaking."

"Mister President," says my favorite aide, Dusty, "the Russians have just nuked Norway."

I stumble down the hall.

The Secretary of Defense tells me the newswires are burning, lights are blinking on all over the war room. They usher me off to Mount Weather. There I watch the world fall apart, orange blossoms exploding around the globe like Pop Secret.

There's only one thing left to do. I get on the phone with my father.

"Dad?"

He mumbles something incomprehensible.

"Sorry," I say. "I couldn't hear you. What was that?"

"I said make it quick."

"We've finally done it, Pop. We've outlasted them all. We didn't miss a thing. We managed to hold off dying right down to the end--to the end of history itself, like you said."

"Who is this?"

"It's me, Hermann."

"I don't have time for this," says my father. "I'm playing Solitaire."

. . .

Out of the Closet
by Michael Price

I should imagine it will come out eventually. I suppose tonight is as good a night as any.

It's just that I have been so terribly lonely as of late, rattling around in this gorgeous old Victorian by myself. And before one might leap to an erroneous conclusion, I would like to make it quite clear that I'm not complaining—truly, no, not in the big picture, anyway. I have been so outrageously fortunate to date—the word *grateful* leaps to mind. Business has been exceptional, money is most certainly not the issue; thank the good Lord for—what I would assume are—rather evident favors. I am so very appreciative of the opportunity to acquire and collect countless beautiful possessions, things that are *to die for*, if you'll excuse the banality of such a stereotypical expression. Mother has, for years, maintained that I have always admired and enjoyed such classic baubles--dating back so very many years to my youth--and she was quite correct; Mother knows me as no others have--so well. I have fashioned my home into my very own personal museum, if you will. And how I love it, I really do. But alone, by myself, which may often leave one with a sinking sense of despondency, detrimental solitude, more and more so as I approach, what should be, the prime of my life. I sometimes consider just how much capital has actually been invested in, what are essentially, costly trinkets. Some exceptionally rare and fabulous pieces I own—yes I do. I make no apologies for any of that; I would do it all again in a second. But recently, I have been finding myself in compelling need of something more, something different, something interminably exciting, in my life.

Another warm and passionate human being might be nice.

And I would be *so* truly remiss if I failed to mention dear Martha—my dear, dearest Martha—she does such a lovely job of maintaining a sense of order in my home, keeping everything so neat and clean when she's here during the week. And I do so value such qualities, above most others, in fact. I honestly have no idea what I would do without her, being away so often as I am.

No misunderstanding, please; the travel is fabulous, even the necessary, often tedious, work related junkets have their singularly charming moments. But I frequently feel like a stranger in my own home, particularly at times such as now, these dreadfully long weekends.

Ooh, baby. Listen to that. Sounds like another bad hair night out there.

I need to stop watching late night cable. Ha!

But I do so tire of... well... hiding, basically. Not coming clean, so to speak. Certainly, I've had more than a few date-mates in my life... although none all that recently, as I think back. Some very lovely young ladies, too—all mistakes, of course, eventually.

Who knew? Whoever knows? Not I, indeed; such has been ruefully demonstrated more than a few times. A real kick in the nards, if I may speak so unrefinedly so late in the day.

Hey, ya know, you take your best shot.

Then...the bombshell drops. And it hurts, too. It really does. No matter who's doing the actual kicking.

I have but a few genuine friends, I suspect—many, many acquaintances, of course--but I believe in earnest that there is not a soul in this world that really *knows* me. Which is undoubtedly my own undoing; I take full responsibility for such a circumstance. I continue to have a difficult time allowing anybody to get close to me; I simply do not let anybody in, I never have. I have always had the tendency to shelter my personal life, my home life, from the rest of society. Lock the door and throw away the key, as they say. It's all so very silly, really—sad, even. I have no idea what I'm so afraid of. It's gotten to be so commonplace, this day and age. It's hard to even see it coming, society scarcely blinks anymore. Or cares, for that matter.

As God is my witness, this is all going to change tonight. It's gonna happen, somehow, some way. Heaven knows, I have waited long enough--the coming-out party to end all coming-out parties.

Am I scared? Silly question, of course I'm scared. This is uncharted territory, all new to me, a first to end all firsts. Tonight, I'm just gonna head down to *Le Chic*, like I've done a thousand times. Except tonight...

Hell, I don't know, maybe everybody already knows. Huh... that would be something. That would almost be a little disappointing—not to mention a rather alarming surprise--at this stage of the game. A bit of a letdown, in a strange and disquieting way.

Ha! Not a chance. *Somebody* is going to be in for the shock of their life tonight. It has to be. At least somebody gotta doesn't know.

That didn't come out quite the way I would have preferred.

Ah well, not to worry.

If this is actually going to happen tonight, I suppose I should start thinking about shaking a leg or two.

What to wear, what to wear... so very many lovely pieces.

Ya know, one of these days, I have got to get in here and... Geez, will you look at all this? I don't even know what's in this damn closet anymo--

. . .

Michael Price *received his BA in Theater from the University of Minnesota in 1980 and, most recently, performed his one-man one-act play No Change of Address at the 2011 MN Fringe Festival. He has been writing fiction, primarily as a source of self-entertainment, for over 30 years.*

The Accidental Florist*
by Marian Brooks

Nora had never so much as plucked a pansy before being hit by an 18 wheeler and suffering a concussion which rewired her brain.

Nora, the lucky owner of a sturdy Honda Accord, walked away from the collision after being hit by the big rig on route 76. However, within a week she was feeling dizzy, had a strange taste in her mouth, slurred speech and migraine headaches.

The doctors diagnosed Nora with post concussion syndrome and prescribed bed rest. Her sister and two children watched as Nora became very weak, lost twenty pounds as well as alarmingly large chunks of her memory.

She had been a research assistant at a pharmaceutical company for the past twenty years. Even as a child, Nora was fascinated by stirring things up. She liked to mix sugar with olive oil or whatever else was on hand just to see what would happen.

Suddenly one morning, Nora woke up almost good as new and stated, "Something's definitely changed." There was an audible pop in her ears. She had a strong craving for mussels in white sauce and discovered, to her horror, that she was not at all interested in mice, beakers or test tubes. She threw her white coats into the trash bin along with her mutilated ID badge after saying goodbye to her friends at PharmaCo.

After some thorny negotiations, Nora received a reasonable settlement from the trucking company. She purchased a new Honda and paid off her children's student loans.

She wrote "thank you" notes to those who sent meals, flowers and cards while she was ill. The flowers, something about the flowers, grabbed her attention and she embraced what was about to become her future.

Elsie Carson had been trying to sell Yellow Tulips for over three years. Nora marched over to Elsie's flower shop and bought herself a business. She kept one employee and began, as if she had always known how, to work with a variety of soils. She knew when to plant bulbs and all about light, temperature and floral arrangements. In the Spring, at the age of 54, Nora opened her shop, "Late Bloomers," much to the surprise of the Garden Club.

*This piece was originally published in The Pittsburgh Flash Fiction Gazette.

• • •

Recently retired **Marian Brooks** has just begun to write some short fiction. Her work has appeared in Curly Red Stories, Post Card Shorts, 50 Word Stories and others.

Toxic
by Lindsey Appleton

"You're nothing, nobody, walk yourself out."
Then you put more of that in your veins
Now didn't you, baby?

You kept me from the intoxicants,
But couldn't protect me from your intoxication,
How could you, baby?

You'd spit your lies and swear them truths.
I was addicted to this, and you were addicted,
Don't you see, baby?

You held me down, held me back, controlled each day.
And what you took from me, took me years to regain.
But I got it back, baby.

I'm not nothing, nobody, and I should have walked out,
Put my pieces back together, got angry, found power.
And stop calling you baby.

• • •

Lindsey D Appleton *was born in California and raised on the island of Hawaii. Attending college at Hawaii Pacific University, she will be graduating May 2013 with a BA in English and a minor in writing. Her poetry and non-fiction have been published in the Rusty Nail, Wanderlust, and Chicken Soup for the Soul. She was the managing editor at Wanderlust, a staff editor for Hawaii Pacific Review, and is the poetry editor for the newly founded Paradise Review.*

Fiction
by e.a.d. sellors

It doesn't pay
to be honest
in this world

It can lose you friends
get you murdered
beaten down

and worst of all
limit your chances
of getting laid.

• • •

6 More Drinks
by Neil Randall

there used to be an old Guinness poster
with a working man in a cloth-cap
hoisting a giant iron girder above his shoulder
 – Guinness for strength.
old boozers used to say
that if you drank 6 pints
you felt as if you could lift that girder, too.
but if you drank six more
you felt as if you'd been hit over the head with it.
I always liked that story.
most of my finest moments have been spent in pubs,
sat in quiet corners on my own,
dreaming, scheming, believing in everything I'm trying
    to do,
letting those first 6 drinks
work through my bloodstream,
inducing a magical parade of genius thoughts,
of secret euphoria and sweet consolation,
along with a warm sense of a love I've not yet known.
after 6 more drinks
the skeletons of all my past failures,
neuroses and hang-ups taunt me.
I feel bloated and beaten, bitter,
unloveable, talentless, a fool parading as a poet,
defeated by a life I've not yet known.
if you're going to try to lift that girder,
be prepared to get hit around the head with it.

. . .

Menace of the Rainbow
by Meg Tuite

I stood before him blasted by the winds of his silent rage. This would be nothing less than a tsunami. I was 35 years old and still there were no trees left standing inside of me. I saw the whitecaps masquerading behind his glasses. His narrowed eyes were pillaging villages as he sat with his hands clasped in his lap. For as long as I could remember this violent turbulence had touched down and torn up this same fragmented single-wide body that I cowered inside, but never thought to move. I just kept working to rebuild the same goddamn ravaged landscape into something salvageable until the next cyclone hit. Flies never gave notice though, before the skies grew dark and vagrant clouds compressed into razor thin lips. I stood my ground as the torsion of my organs wrenched themselves into opposing forces of cell migration between malignant or benign, dwelling or scrap metal.

* * * *

You know girl, you have no gust. I simply look right through a sprinkler of my mom who squalled and nipped at me. I don't give a shit about a downpour here or there when I cover myself with the windbreaker of you. I watch you rambling around this district of us with some kind of buoyancy. What the hell is that? If I ever engulfed myself in the gale of dad's lack of air and mom's boisterous torment, I'd be an outline of the space that once shackled us. So, look at me, not through me. I will fill you up and watch sheets of you rain down in a monsoon that drowns us. I never asked for the sun to bruise our skin with its tedium. "Baby, I've got the taste of you swallowing me up, so don't get all drizzly on me now. I am hemorrhaging a frenzied lightning that is toxic with the quickening beat of its thunder under my skin."

* * * *

My mouth wrenched open its shoddy door that always stuck. The air took on a thick and sinister stillness. The eye of my family and friends were steady before the storm. Why don't these assholes get out of hurricane alley? Why do they bleed themselves over this skeletal territory that will only become obliterated year after year? There is something threatening about a stretch of open terrain with no history, no tooth decay.

My gums had unoccupied spaces. A history, blow by blow, of enduring agitation, the smack of waves upon boulders that one listens to day after day without even registering, and yet without it there would be an absence of potency.

I looked at this man who had traced the lines of my face with a gun. My neck had wedded itself to the contours of his guillotine archway of compressed fingers. He sat in his recliner while whitecaps sprayed from his pores. "Come here, baby," he said. My fists became two restraining orders as I moved towards him. I sunk down to my knees. His fingers slid along the sides of my twitching cheeks. I put my head in his lap. "God, baby," I said. "How could I ever live without you."

. . .

Meg Tuite's writing has appeared in numerous journals including Berkeley Fiction Review, 34th Parallel, Epiphany, One, the Journal, Monkeybicycle and Boston Literary Magazine. She has been nominated several times for the Pushcart Prize. She is the fiction editor of The Santa Fe Literary Review and Connotation Press. She is the author of Domestic Apparition (2011) San Francisco Bay Press, Implosion (2013) Sententia Books and her chapbooks, Disparate Pathos,(2012) Monkey Puzzle Press and Reverberations (2012) Deadly Chaps Press. She has a monthly column, Exquisite Quartet, published up at Used Furniture Review. The Exquisite Quartet Anthology-2011 is available.
Her blog: http://megtuite.wordpress.com.

A Cracker Ambush

by Bob Kalkreuter

Albert stopped rocking when he saw two figures coming through the scrub-brush at the edge of the pine forest. At first they looked like sticks, growing taller and more defined as they approached, barely visible through the sun-mottled foliage of the western trees.

"James, you expecting somebody?" he asked, pointing.

His son looked, squinted, shook his head. "I don't see nobody," he said.

Since James was so near-sighted, Albert didn't expect him to see anything. But Florida in 1884 was still wild, and Albert was wary of strangers, even though the last Seminole uprising was over twenty-five years ago.

And people didn't just show up at the farm without warning. Nobody he wanted to see anyway.

"Just wondered if you're looking for somebody, is all," said Albert. "Appears to be two, headed our way."

"Can't say," said James, tugging on the brim of his round, floppy hat.

"What do you mean, you can't say? You expecting somebody or not?"

"Well, I don't guess it matters. If they're coming, we'll know soon enough."

"It matters a lot. You don't know who's out there roaming around nowadays," said Albert. He'd been born in the mine country of Kentucky, and moved to the west coast of Florida in 1860. After buying several acres of land near the Manatee River, he managed to convert the wild scrub into usable farmland, working fifteen hours a day, by himself. Three years later he married Martha Rutland and they had two sons, James and Reuben.

Martha came from a large family that raised cattle near the community of Myakka. Albert met her while buying three cows from her father.

From the beginning, Martha's father was against the marriage. He didn't think Albert's farm would be large enough to support his only daughter. But Martha was a head-strong woman, and she pushed ahead despite her father's warning.

For seven years they worked together, building the farm. Happy years, for Albert. Then in 1870, Martha and Reuben both died of diphtheria. Reuben was four, James six. After that, Albert and James lived on the farm alone, raising cows, corn, and sweet potatoes, which Albert traded among the neighbors for additional food and supplies. Except for rare visits to let James visit with his grandparents, Albert had little contact with his father-in-law.

Now, James sat looking into the distance with eyes that could see no farther than the front yard. He shook his head. "They ain't going to be no problem," he said.

"How do you know that? I heard the postmaster got ambushed and killed Saturday. Charles Abbe. You heard about that?"

"No," said James. "I ain't."

Through the tree tops the sun glowed like a furnace, and the air was warm, even in late December.

"Rumor has it, Charlie Willard killed him," said Albert. He was smoking a hand-rolled cigarette and flicked ashes down on the porch planking.

"Charlie Willard?"

"Yeah. I saw you talking to him last week, down at Bidwell's store."

"Charlie? He's all right. Drinks a bit, but he ain't going to hurt us."

"They're looking for him pretty hard, I hear," said Albert.

"Who is?"

"Sheriff Watson's got men all over Manatee County, looking for him."

James looked around, his eyes flickering. "Well..." he said. "I don't know nothing about that."

As the distant figures grew into men, they continued to advance with strong, steady strides, white men, whoever they were, and Albert's senses, honed by years in the Florida scrub, warned him to be cautious. "One of them's got a shotgun," he said. He rose a little too fast and flinched against the sharp pain in his back.

"Hunters, more'n likely," said James, tilting his head to catch the afternoon sunlight on the brim of his floppy hat. "Just lost."

"We don't know that."

"We don't need to be worried."

"Well, go in and get the shotgun anyway," said Albert.

James didn't move. "Charlie ain't going to hurt us."

"What do you mean, Charlie?" Albert turned toward him. "What do you know? Is that Charlie Willard?"

"Could be, I suppose."

"What's Charlie Willard doing here, James?"

"He ain't going to hurt us. We're not rich Yankees, trying to buy up all the land. He just wants to make the county safe for us Crackers."

"Safe for... My God, is that what he told you? You don't believe..."

James peered out from under his hat brim. "He's on our side," he said. "He wants to help poor farmers like us."

In the side yard was a small, wheel-less wagon, partially scraped and painted and upturned in a clump of yellowed sand spurs. Behind the house, partially visible, was a horse barn.

"Charlie only wants to help himself. Tell me you weren't part of this, James. It's... it's murder." He flipped the stub of his cigarette across the porch and onto the sandy ground just beyond the railing.

"We need more land. Like Grandpa's got in Myakka. We need to get it before the Yankees buy it all up."

"More land? Your Grandpa needs land to run all his cattle."

"We've got cows too."

"Four? We've got plenty of land for that."

"Four's not enough. I want a real herd."

"I don't know how we'd work it, if we got more land," said Albert. "Just the two of us, we're doing all we can do to keep up now."

"I can do it, Pa. You don't work half what I do, now.

"Since I fell from that damn horse, I can't do much of anything. My back..." He tried to straighten and grimaced.

"I'm used to hard work. Just turn the farm over to me. I'll do it. We'll get more land and bring in cattle."

Albert sighed. "It's money we don't have, James."

"We can make it, with more cattle."

"No, James. We can't afford it."

"You just don't want to. Grandpa will loan us the money. He told me..."

Albert shook his head. "No, I can't do that. I'm not putting myself in debt..." He wanted to say *in debt to William Rutland*, but he caught himself and stopped.

"It ain't just you, Pa. It's me, too. This is my place, too."

Albert glanced up to see the strangers getting closer, tramping around a Palmetto thicket. "You ain't even full grown yet. I put in fifteen hours a day, working to make this farm. And soon as my back's better..."

"Charlie said he knew folks who'd help for a couple months."

"Charlie Willard? The murderer?"

James stood. He looked straight ahead, in the general direction of the yard, but Albert knew the men were still too far away for James to see.

"I told him we'd put him up a couple days," said James. "That's all. In the barn. Him and Joe Anderson. Till this blows over."

"You told him... what?"

"We'd put them up in the barn. That's all. Just till it blows over."

"James, what's got into you? We can't do that!"

"Why not, Pa? It'll blow over soon. We can't abandon them. Not after what they did for us."

"For us? They didn't do anything for us. They killed Charles Abbe, James. Killed him!"

"Abbe and those like him, they're buying up all the property. Pretty soon, they're going to crowd the rest of us right out."

Albert was standing behind the rocker. His head whirled, as if he were dizzy. "They're criminals, James. Criminals!"

"Howdy," called one of the strangers, stopping between a pair of mango trees about 30 yards from the house. He raised his hand in greeting.

Albert studied the men. He didn't recognize either one. Although he was used to the irregular way most men dressed, they wore clothes so mismatched, they might have been stolen from a traveling circus.

"You seen Joe Anderson?" asked one of the men. He was tall, but his britches were so short he could have waded into ankle-deep water without getting them wet. A pistol was wedged under his belt. A long-bladed knife hung in a sheath at his side.

"Joe Anderson?" said Albert, glancing at James, who was squinting at the men, his lips tight.

The second man was short, with thin, unruly hair. He held a double-barrel shotgun in the crook of his arm. His ratty, suspendered britches were held in place by a length of frayed twine. He had a thick, reddish mustache and sideburns.

"The sheriff sent us around to see if we can flush him out," said the shotgun man. "Him and Charlie Willard, they killed the postmaster over near Sarasota Bay."

"I ain't seen Charlie in months," said James, rubbing his thigh.

"We ain't looking for Charlie," said the tall man. "We already got him. We're looking for Joe Anderson."

James sat down and stared, tight-lipped and silent.

"If you know anybody mixed up in this, you need to let us know," said the tall man. He touched the knife sheath at his belt. "You don't need to worry about any of that scum coming back on you. We're going to round them all up. Already picked up some, and they're talking."

"Well," said Albert. "We don't know nothing." In the distance, the sun slithered between the jig-sawed pine branches, winking like a jewel sliding down into a pocket of the earth. "It's an awful thing, killing a man like that."

"Yeah, it's an awful thing all right," said the tall man. He shifted his feet and looked from Albert to James and back again.

James looked away.

The short man with the reddish mustache and sideburns shifted the butt of his shotgun to the ground. "You're a good man, Albert," he said, leaning forward. "But this here killing has a lot of people riled."

"Me'n James here don't know nothing about it."

"I don't reckon you remember me," said the short man, fingering the shotgun barrel. "Name's Rutland. George Rutland. Martha's cousin. I saw you at the funeral, but you had other things... I didn't want to bother you."

Albert studied him closely. A slight breeze kicked up a dust bunny in the yard, whipping around the wagon tongue lying upended in the yard. "No... I don't remember," he said, frowning.

"Frank here's my neighbor," said George, nodding at the tall man. "We came over this way cause we heard..." He looked at James.

Albert was silent, and James seemed to be staring into space.

"Well, we know Charlie Willard's a friendly guy and likes to talk, particularly when he's drunk..." said George.

"Which is most of the time," said Frank.

"That's so," said George. "And most of what he says ain't worth repeating." Here he stopped talking, as if he wanted the words to take on additional weight. "Long as he's the only one saying it, nobody much'll be paying attention."

"What's he saying?" said Albert.

"One of my cousins is a deputy," said George. "I'd hate to see any of Martha's kin be brought into this mess. I heard the newspapers is even nosing around."

"What's he saying?" asked Albert again.

"Anderson may be headed this way."

"Well, he ain't coming to see us," said Albert. "Is he James?"

James shook his head. "No sir," he said. "He ain't."

"We didn't say he was coming right here, to your place. Just this part of the county," said Frank.

George nodded. "If Anderson was around, where do you think he'd hide? You know, based on what you know about the land."

There was a long silence while they all looked around the yard, each at something different.

"Well," said Albert, reaching to touch James on the shoulder. "There's lots of places…"

"There is," said George. "Too many to know for sure. But if you was to guess. You know, maybe a couple places. He needs to be brought in, Albert."

Another silence.

"You know the woods around here, James," said Albert. "Where do you think somebody might hide?"

A Mockingbird trilled a string of unconnected songs.

"Well, if it was me," said James, waiting for the Mockingbird to fall silent. "I might look at Turner's old cabin. It ain't been used in years, but it's a good place." He motioned off toward the sun dropping behind the trees. "It's close to the river, the way you came. But that's just me. I don't know where he'd go."

"Can you show us?"

"We got a cow fixing to calve. I need to be here."

"Well, can you tell us where it is, then."

"Sure," said James.

That evening, Albert sat at the table, smoking. An empty supper plate sat in front of him. "You did the right thing," he said, blowing a thin stream of smoke toward the ceiling.

Light from a lantern at the edge of the table flickered yellow among the shadows.

"What's that?" said James.

"Joe Anderson. Telling them where to find him."

James reached to fill his glass from a jug of water. "I don't have no idea where he is," he said. "Except that he ain't at Turner's old cabin."

Albert watched his son, smoked. "You're pretty well grown now," he said.

James looked at him and smiled. "I reckon so."

"There was a time, it was my job to protect you."

"You're my Pa," said James. "We stick together. Help each another. Like on the farm here."

"It ain't my job to protect you anymore. Now, I just want to."

"You don't have to protect me at all, Pa."

A gust of wind rattled around the edges of the window, working inside, under the door.

"Sounds like a storm kicking up," said James.

"Your cousin will be back. If not tonight, tomorrow," said Albert.

"It ain't my fault, if they don't find him."

"And when they come back," said Albert. "You're not going to be here."

There was a silent moment while they measured each other.

"Where do you think I'm going?"

"I won't have a murderer living under my roof."

James jumped up, his cheeks flushing. He spread his hands on the table. "I'm no murderer! I didn't kill nobody!"

"Not directly. But you had a hand in it, even if you only knew about it."

James stood with his feet planted. He pointed at Albert. "You're throwing me out? Is that what you're trying to do?"

"I'm not throwing you out, as my son. Only as a murderer."

"I didn't murder anybody," said James, his voice slightly strident.

"If you're protecting him, you're part of what he is."

"I didn't do nothing!"

"As my son, you're welcome to stay. As a murderer, James, I won't have…"

"What if I refuse to go?" said James. He drew himself straight, tensing. "You going to force me?"

They both stopped for a moment and listened to rain clicking against the roof and windows.

"Not physically. Not with my back."

"Even if you didn't have a bad back…"

"James, it's your choice. If you're here when they come back. *When* they come back. You'll have to explain what happened. I won't cover for you. You going to have me murdered too?"

James looked at him hard, then sat down and cocked his head, as if trying to hear the drumbeat of rain. "I ain't running."

"Maybe you didn't pull the trigger. But what you're doing, it's going to bring you right into the middle of it… Can't you see?"

"You expect me to go out in this storm?" James gestured toward the door.

"No murderer's staying in my house, James. Storm or no storm."

"I'm no murderer."

"Well you can wait for your cousin then… Explain it to him."

"Maybe I don't want to stay anyway," said James, glancing toward the window, where the rain ran up the glass in an uneven wave. "You just want to get rid of me because I want to get more land."

"You want to live on the run?"

"Grandpa will let me stay there."

"If you're involved in murder?"

"I'm not involved in murder!"

"Then tell the sheriff your story, and help them track down Anderson before it's too late to help yourself."

They were both very still as the wind and rain raged in the darkness.

"So you want me to turn on Joe Anderson?" said James.

"You're not turning on him. He killed a man."

James sat down and pushed the edge of his empty supper plate. He put his elbows on the table, lacing his fingers to support his chin. He spoke slowly. "You want me to go against everything I believe."

"You can believe anything you want. But when you cross over into murder to defend it, you're wrong and you become a murderer, just like Anderson and Willard."

Lightning zigzagged in the darkness, brightening the window. A few seconds later, thunder cracked and rolled into the trailing darkness.

"Those poor bastards," said James, smiling. "If they didn't make Turner's old cabin before the rain broke…"

"They'll be soaked anyway," said Albert, smiling as well. "The roof on that old cabin's been shot for years."

"Yeah," said James, laughing. "They'll be good and soaked."

Elements
by Kimberly Zook

My years as an organic chemist have taught me only one thing: every human on earth has a single element that permeates their entire being. Unfortunately, I'm still trying to discover mine.

MERCURY (Hg) - My husband's metallic body pools into a heavy liquid over mine as he falls asleep on top of me under the hot Nicaraguan sun. Beads of quicksilver drip into my pores. A restless scorpion stirs under the roof of our hut. My lungs dampen to a level of toxicity when my suave Latin lover rolls off my body.

I do not miss the vapors of winter in the states. Are my sisters thinking of their ex-pat sibling baking in a hut on a dual-volcanic island shaped like an hour-glass, waiting...

We married only three weeks after magnetically meeting on the shore of Lake Managua. Its waters drip of mercury. Our honeymoon, a ferry ride over waters buzzing of bull sharks, ended at Ometepe Island, Raul's home.

"I used to race those sharks as a boy," Raul told me, "but they're unpredictable and aggressive. You're lucky they didn't catch me."

Volatile mercury, known for speed and mobility among the Roman gods, should be handled with care.

MANGANESE (Mn) - Her hard and brittle calluses crackle in my hand. Raul's mother snorts and returns to flattening tortillas on plantain leaves in the spicy kitchen. My efforts at making tortillas do little to melt this manganese mother. Our relationship, it is tainted with rust. My kidneys ache of her element.

"Mi carina, Zobeida," she exclaims at the entrance of a dazzling young woman. *My dear, Zobeida.*

"Quien es que?" Zobeida asks as a little girl peers around her legs. *Who is that?*

The disgust in his mother's voice burns my face. "Raul's esposa." *Raul's wife.*

"Esposa," spats Zobeida. Her eyes reflect a painful shock before she shrugs it away. "Puede cocinar?" *Can she cook?*

Raul's mother cackles and tosses her head to the black stove where my lumpy thick tortillas burn next to her fluffy light ones. At the table, Zobeida begins to sort through a pile of black beans, casting aside the ones bored into by insects.

The forgotten little girl stares up at me, her coffee-rich almond eyes linger on my necklace of cowrie shells.

Raul's been gone for six days now, off to Managua with a cart full of plantains. My passionate drunken love for him begins to dissipate as the bruises of manganese upon my body color to a shade of amethyst.

Manganese colors glass a shade of amethyst, which was once believed to protect a person from intoxication.

MAGNESIUM (Mg) - The little girl giggles as I wrinkle up my nose at the stench of a stink bug. We've been harvesting coffee all afternoon. I've learned only that her name is Maria and she is six years old. I anticipate Raul's return, so I can understand more about her.

Maria's delicate thin fingers wrap around my wrist, preventing me from accidentally disturbing another pungent bug. Her infectious laughter and brilliant smile have healed my wounds from this morning's interactions in the kitchen, and I relax in the shade of the tall coffee plants.

"Papa!" Maria shouts.

She bursts into the air like an exploding vision of fireworks, and races down the row of plants. I glance up from my basket of red coffee berries to find Raul walking toward us. I look past him but see no one. Raul gets down on one knee and Maria steps up and jumps into his arms, a move so smooth it's been long-practiced.

His free hand grabs my waist and pulls me to his body.

"My daughter, you met," he states.

"Mi papa," Maria says proudly.

"They live with us, some days."

"They?" I ask, stepping away from his magnetic pull.

"Maria and her mother, Zobeida."

My body hardens. Raul sees the accusation in my glare.

"She's not my girlfriend. You now are my wife." Raul slowly reaches down for my hand. "My wife, I love."

The instant drain of attraction for Raul leaves my body quaking as his last words sprinkle down on me like rain drops on a cracked desert floor.

I panic, running blind inside the labyrinth of my mind until Maria's hand gently touches my shoulder. She leans out of Raul's arms towards me and lightly touches the seashells around my neck.

"I make."

Supernova magnesium, she ricochets the essence of life into the universe, making it impossible to escape.

• • •

Kimberly Zook *is currently working on a collection of short stories based on her experiences of living in a tropical rainforest. Her writing has earned first and third place in writing contests hosted by Mom Writer's Literary Magazine and WOW! Women on Writing. Kimberly is a military wife and a mother of three daughters. She blogs at Zook Book Nook.*
http://www.kimberlyzook.com

Skylark
by February Grace

I was captured by a voice
a skylark's laughter-no-a sparrow, she
taking wing and with the draft flown upward
My heart aloft; tattooed upon her breast
all feathered softness
wherever on this earth her feet may fall
though I remain, I am just hers.

Poet
by February Grace

How lifeless blood itself can feel
when running cold through marrow breached
by dark command, to withdraw prose
from poet's soul without consent.

Speechless
by February Grace

Speak? I cannot speak, yet
would if in so doing
past the hitch within my throat
I could force sound.
Wrest by violence the voice
from cords which tie it;
speak of hair so dark and
eye so deep no light escapes, yet
is absorbed
just to reflect upon my face.

. . .

February Grace *is a writer, poet, and artist who lives somewhere that is much colder than she'd like most of the time. Her debut novel, GODSPEED, was released in 2012. You can find her on Twitter @FebruaryGrace, or visit her blog: www.februarywriter.blogspot.com*

Movie Star
by Alan Haider

Light pulses through the frames
as they speed from reel to real.

Thousands of stationary pictures
coalesce as a storyline. The stars

are aligned. If only for one night.
And the movie is more real than

the night sky: a black sheet
pin-pricked with light from a

million miles away. I am in the
movie, even though I am not a

star. I have no lines, but I
speak with my eyes, telling the

world I am alive. I wonder if I
have already burned out, and I

am just watching a me light years
away that has already disappeared.

. . .

Alan Haider *is an emerging writer who currently resides in South Florida, where he was born and raised. His work has appeared—or will appear soon—in print publications such as Turbulence, Star*Line, and Bête Noire, and in various zines online.*

D.B.
by Kathryn Lynch

I

Some people knew instinctively how to relax. But for the Old Lady, in her second year of retirement, it was a newly acquired skill. Many years of long hours on the job had always suited her intense personality. Making the adjustment to a slower paced life had been difficult, but she had done it.

Every afternoon she stretched out in a lawn chair with a book, earphones piping Mozart or Beethoven into her core. Sometimes she slept, the sun gently warming the area, breezes streaming through the redwoods keeping her cool.

She was not alone. A large bullmastiff lay faithfully at her feet, snoring loudly when he slept. At times the dog wandered back into the woods to see what he could find, but he always returned to his favorite spot. Although he now weighed more than 100 pounds, the Old Lady never regretted rescuing him as a puppy from a box in front of the grocery store. They were buddies.

II

One afternoon, when the Old Lady awoke from a short nap, she realized that the dog was out of sight. He did not respond to her calls as he usually did. It was their routine to end the sunbathing by going into the house where she would feed him his dinner. He loved to eat and it worried her that he had not returned.

As the sun began to fade, she spotted him at the edge of the clearing, coming out of the woods. He was struggling to drag a very large object which he finally deposited at her feet.

The temperature inside the old lady suddenly dropped. At the same time she began to sweat, beads of salty water dripping down the sides of her face. She could hear the sound of her own breathing, gasping, gulping noises.

The dog was chewing contentedly on the forearm and hand of a human being. The bones looked dried and yellowed, old. Whatever happened, had taken place a long time ago. There was certainly no need for an ambulance. She decided not to call the police until she had thought this through. Placing the bones in a garbage bag, she hid them under her car in the driveway.

III

The next day she and the dog set out into the woods at the spot where the Old Lady had seen the animal emerge with the bones. She wore heavy boots and carried a small hatchet to ease her progress forward.

The forested area on her property was tangled by decades of uninterrupted growth. She had never explored it, content to enjoy its raw beauty instead of attempting to control it in any way. Redwoods grew everywhere, most more than 100 feet tall. The undergrowth was interspersed with fallen tree trunks, heavy growths of ferns, blackberries, and puddles of standing water. It was slow going.

The Old Lady kept her eyes open for more bones, but she saw none. Had she not stumbled onto the building, she would have missed it. It was approximately 10 feet by 12 feet, constructed from old wood, complete with a door. It lay camouflaged between two redwoods, access complicated by blackberries which had encircled the structure several times over.

After chopping through the growth at the entrance, the door opened with a chilling squeak. Spiders ran in every direction, two or three small lizards scrambled for quick cover. Tree frogs on the walls croaked in unison. A black rat ran past the Old Lady's legs, chased by the dog.

It was rudimentary but livable. And someone had indeed lived there, but not recently, judging from the cobwebs which hung down and crisscrossed the area in every direction. A small woodstove stood by the back wall, its pipes angling upwards and out of the building near the roof. Next to the stove was a supply of wood ready to burn. In the corner, was a mat covered by several blankets. The Old Lady pictured a bearded hermit preparing for the night, listening for unfriendly sounds before he closed his eyes.

A hand hewn table held a couple of dishes, a cup, and a spoon. Next to the dishes was a large black carrying bag. Carefully banging on the bag so that the spiders would leave first, she opened the cover to look inside. To her shock and delight, the bag was full of money. Now she shoved packages of cash into her pants pockets and went home with the dog.

IV

She had grabbed two bundles of 50-$20.00 bills held together with rubber bands; the money was in good shape, though the bills had been printed in 1969.

The Old Lady went to Google on the Internet, searching for "missing 1969 money". The answer came quickly.

In 1971, Northwest Orient Airlines had paid a $200,000.00 ransom (all in $20.00 bills) to a hijacker who had parachuted from the rear stairs of their 727 jet plane into the night with the money. It was widely believed that the hijacker had died on impact, probably in Washington or Oregon. Extensive searches failed to find him or the cash. In 1980 an eight year old boy had found $5,880.00 of the cash badly deteriorated by the side of the Columbia River. The hijacker and the rest of the money were not to be found.

The serial numbers of the missing money had been listed on the site. After much checking, the Old Lady knew that she had found the rest of the cash. The bullmastiff had found D.B. Cooper, at least parts of him, which were wrapped in a garbage bag in her carport. He had not died on impact, but much later from causes which would probably never be determined.

V

Now she went daily to the cabin, dragging back as much of the money as she could. On the fifth day she completed the job, removing the black bag as well, closing the door and leaving the structure to the reinvasion of the blackberries and the spiders. It was her intention not to revisit the area.

After replacing all of the old rubber bands around the money with new ones, the Old Lady burned the airline bag and the old bands in her woodstove. The cash, all $194,120.00 of it, lay nestled in four environmentally friendly "green bags" which she had purchased for a dollar apiece at the grocery store.

She knew that dealing with banks was out of the question. Scanning just one serial number would inform a teller that it was a hijacked money bill. She decided to visit large cities about four times a year, paying her hotel bill on checkout, shopping in large busy discount stores, eating in fine restaurants, gambling in the casinos, and then leaving town. It helped that the money was in $20.00 bills which drew little attention. It would take a day or two for the businesses to deposit their accounts receivable into corporate bank accounts.

By then, some of the cash would have been redistributed to customers as change and circulated once again. Either way, she would be long gone.

The Old Lady carefully placed the bag with the bones in the outgoing garbage pickup. Whenever the dog returned with a bone or two over the next few weeks, she repeated the process, except for the skull. When the dog deposited it at her feet, the Old Lady gave in to the temptation to keep a souvenir. "D.B" sat on a shelf of lush green house plants in her living room. When she passed by in the morning, she always greeted the man who had brought some excitement into her life and into the business of being retired.

Epilogue: The FBI had revised their evaluation of D.B. Cooper. He had survived the jump and he was passing the money in large cities in Washington, Oregon, and California. They had placed age-enhanced photos of Cooper at the cash registers of large businesses in these cities, but he did not return to the same locations. Agents estimated that Cooper was at least 75 years old but he was still outsmarting them at every turn. About one quarter of the money had been circulated to date.

The Old Lady enjoyed her trips out of town, but after two or three days she was always ready to return home. She missed D.B. She thought that D.B. must be lonely, waiting on the shelf for them to come back. "What do you think?" she asked her companion. The aging dog lying on the passenger seat next to her snored loudly, but at the sound of her voice, he wagged his tail.

. . .

Biker Queen Fishing Story
by Timmy Reed

My neighbor dragged me fishing, like bait. He wanted me to do business with his "best buddy", an attorney out west where I maybe wanted some land. I didn't know what I wanted. The guy was a Mormon or something. The whole thing was weird. I didn't get to know him. But I could tell he had problems. We all have problems. And it turns out fishing was mostly waiting and drinking, which was pretty much what I expected but worse. I would've given a fortune to have ants injected in my veins, if only for the excitement. The only thrill on the water was an emasculated ranger threatening a group of teens who were throwing themselves off a cliff like members of a suicide cult.

When we were done trying to fool the fishes, I insisted we have another drink before the long ride back home. Part of me hoped I would pass out before then and they would just tuck me into the backseat of my neighbor's SUV and wake me when we were in my driveway. My neighbor and his buddy were reluctant but they finally agreed to stop at a bar & grill near the reservoir. The parking lot, bar, patio, and surrounding territory was full of bikers and their girlfriends. It was a Rally! They all looked like they were having a great time. Like they had been having a great time all day. A much better time than we'd had sitting out on that mud-filled lake.

At the bar, I drank a lot very quickly it felt like. It's hard to tell. The sun had been so hot out there; I really was in a daze. I told my companions I was stumbling because of the rocking of the boat on the reservoir, which was basically the City's glass of water and no choppier than a puddle.

I admired the bikers. They didn't have to go home to their nagging wives or dull girlfriends; their fun wives and party-hearty girlfriends were right here with them, egging them on. Hitting the open road. Grilling chunks of dinosaur meat. Dancing to loud rock and roll music. But mostly drinking outside on picnic tables.

The prettiest of the girls at the rally was barely eighteen. Her lips were like raspberries about to spoil. I disgusted myself just thinking about her. I have two daughters. One of them is dead. The other is all grown up. We're all all grown up.

I wasn't interested in raspberry-lipped infants, I wanted to meet a real woman. A woman my age. A woman I could have conceivably married years ago if we both had lived different lives. I ordered a large steak and another shot - my second and the food hadn't even come yet, my neighbor pointed out.

"I need it," I told him, mumbled something about "sea legs."

I scanned the party like a sailor desperate for the temptations of a harbor town. My neighbor's buddy, the attorney, noticed me.

"Watcha lookin' for?" I don't mean to write him so hickish, but that's the closest I can get to what he sounded like on paper. I sound like water being sucked down a drain. Why fight it?

"I'm searching out the Biker Queen," I said. "The Matriarch."

I looked deeper into the party. A mass appeared on the horizon. Flesh. And leather. And smoke. I hopped up from the table.

I'd found her.

She was holding court in back.

She was not the oldest at the bar, but she was close to it and she was by dog shits the meanest looking. The alpha-female. That's what I was looking for. I wondered for a second if she had gotten her status from being the alpha male's woman, but I pushed the thought from my head and with tipsy aplomb sort of danced in her direction, too drunk to be embarrassed about my Hawaiian shirt. A gift from my wife's awful mother.

The Biker Queen was about twelve feet tall it looked and as wide as a tank. Motorcycles zipped around her like flies around a record-breaking bovine turd. The sexy old hag had long hair, black and white like the movies. Young blonde wet tee shirt contest losers clung to her Viking braids like burrs in a golden retriever's mane. Her tattoos were ancient runes and vomiting bald eagles, battleships straddled by the grim reaper, swastikas dining on elves' blood. She wore a crown of barbed wire and a ripped tank top that read: "I don't need a helmet, YOU DO!" If I'd had better judgment or wasn't so dissatisfied with my life on earth, I would've worn one to approach her.

I pushed across the tented dance floor and covered myself with biker sweat in the process. At the far end she sat on two oversized picnic tables, flanked by a pair of salivating grey wolves. Heat radiated from her leather pants and nearly blew me back to my table where I was supposed to be waiting for a shitty steak I didn't even want. I was supposed to be back there dreading the prospect more than death of the long drive back with my neighbor and his Mormon(?) to see my wife, a wife that felt more like a genetic condition than someone who wanted to share her fleeting time on earth with me. The feeling was mutual. I fought through the crowd, still dancing, now holding two light beers.

When I got up close, the Biker Queen turned out to be three times as big as she had looked from across the dance floor. I had to borrow a microphone from the deejay who was too busy bonging beers and blowing the foam out on the bare tits in the crowd to notice. I could only imagine what my neighbor was thinking.

"Hello!" I screamed, tugging on one of her leg hairs. Boy, was I feeling ballsy. "I am a lonely fisherman!"

"Did I hear something?!" Tables turned over when she spoke.

"YES! You heard ME! A lonely fisherman who hates to fish and is dissatisfied with his current and longtime situation in life!"

She now saw me and scooped me up in her palm, brought me close to eye level.

"Little Man," she said. She scratched me on my bald, sunburned head with one of her spiky rings. "You do not look like a fisherman."

"Well, thanks," I said. "I'm not really."

"You look like a fish. You don't even look like a fish. You look like a tadpole, blind to the murky world around you."

"That's true!" I said. It was hard not to agree with her. "I loved my life at one time! But I was only a little boy and many years have passed since then! Now I am old and blind! And bored and boring! Marry me!"

The Biker Queen laughed so loud that for a second I was afraid her mate would hear and come stomping through the forest from wherever he was and skin me, then use my bones as toothpicks. But I was too caught up in the moment to give fear a chance.

"So...Is that a 'No'?" I asked.

"No!" she roared. I nearly fell off her hand. "That's a YES! Take me home and bed me now or regret this moment and the rest of your life forever!"

If this had been a cartoon and not real life, I would've gulped or at least said, "Gulp."

Instead, I said "Fuck."

This is why I said "Fuck": I love my wife. In fact, after twenty-five years, it would be impossible to love myself, or even tolerate myself, without loving my wife. I know that. And I know that I am afraid to be anything but plainly unhappy because I don't know how. I would rather be comfortable than change. If the grass is green, it turns brown when I get near it.

What I didn't know was how to marry a biker queen, let alone have sex with one, or live in her sidecar and make her happy. I wanted to though. Or, part of me did. I wanted to crawl in her earlobe and build a nest, hoist my pirate flag and sleep on a bed of golden wax with the sound of engines roaring and the wild country whipping past like outside an open freight car. Not because I loved her, but because I hated what I had become.

"Are you okay, Little Man?"

"I'm not sure." I had to admit it.

All she did was laugh, long and slow, careful not to let me fall even though the earth was shaking.

"Could you give me a ride home?" I asked. "I can't stand the guys I came here with."

"You don't have to marry me, Little Man." Her smile let me know that life would continue whether I had anything to do with it or not. And everything was back to normal again. Until her husband rolled up on top of an enormous dust cloud, followed by what looked like some lost tribe of Neanderthal warriors. Then I truly wished that I had not gone fishing, but had stayed at home where I belong.

. . .

Timmy Reed *is a writer from Baltimore, Maryland. He worked as an Editorial Intern at Crazyhorse and his writing has recently appeared in Everyday Genius, Gone Lawn, Spilt Milk Magazine, Pure Slush, The Bicycle Review, The Rusty Nail, and others. He was awarded Third Place in the 2011 Baltimore City Paper Fiction Contest. He has stories forthcoming in Connotation Press, Black Heart Magazine, Cobalt Review, and the print anthology, gorge. He blogs about animals and stuff at* http://underratedanimals.wordpress.com/ *and writes tiny stories on Twitter @BMORETIMMYREED*

Between Princess and Power Queens
by Kate O'Reilley

My entire life has been spent drifting in the ocean. Since I was a child, the creatures of the sea have accepted and nurtured me. I have never wanted anything else. But as I mature from a young girl into a grown woman, the sun and the moon signal to me that I must leave the protection of my deep, blue world and move to land. They tell me that I need to become like other women.

For as long as I can remember, I have frolicked in the warm water between two islands. I have stared at these landmasses for decades, watching the sun rise above one and set behind the other. As I look off to the east, the Island of Power Queens pierces the water and rises majestically from the sea. I spin around to look behind me and, to the west, the Island of Princesses sparkles and shines on the horizon. My legs and arms are growing weary from a lifetime of striving to stay afloat. Maybe the wisdom of the moon and sun are correct, and it's time to find a new home.

The thought of which island to choose overwhelms and terrifies me. I know so little about either of them. Diving under water, I twirl in circles until I'm dizzy. The soothing ocean water wraps around my skin and holds me close. Once I am completely disoriented, I propel my head out into the open air but keep my eyes held tightly shut. When I open them, my decision will be made for me. Whichever isle I spot first is the one I will select as my new home. I know it's a shameful and cowardly approach to make such an important determination. However, I find either option so entirely intimidating and menacing, it seems like the best solution. With trepidation, I slowly open my eyes. Initially, the bright rays of sunshine reflecting off the ocean's surface blind me. It takes me a moment to realize that the bright rays are not only emanating from the sun, but also from glimmers of light reflecting off of the shiny Princess Island and all of its glittery, noble things.

I gather up my remaining energy and swim toward Princess Island. As I reach shore, I instantly spot hundreds of women. At least I think they are women. They seem to have the same anatomical parts as I do, but somehow they are very different. Their legs are long and elegant. Mine are short, muscular, firm and bulky. The princesses' breasts are round, firm, large, and they almost stand up straight off their chests. In comparison, mine are small and sort of saggy. Every princess has the appearance of a woman in her twenties, even the ones whose necks and hands are weathered and have the wrinkled texture of a much older woman. The skin and features on their faces are tight, creating the impression that they are all caught head on in a stiff offshore breeze. With my wrinkles, freckles and sunspots, I am an instant standout. Imperfections and flaws define me, just as they are defined by the opposite.

Feeling conspicuous, I hesitantly approach one of them. "Excuse me," I say softly, unsure how to speak their language. "Can you help me? I've been treading water my entire life. I need to move to land and find a place where I fit in." The princess just stares blankly as she blinks her painted eyes at me. I plead with her, "Please, please can you help me? Can you tell me how to fit in?" There is no hint of emotion or empathy upon her face. In fact, there is no evidence of any sort of facial expression. At long last, she speaks and her tone is snotty, condescending, and mocking, "Only Princesses are allowed on the beach. You'll contaminate things. You must leave at once." Her lips are the only part of her face that moves when she speaks. Her eyes, nose, forehead and cheeks appear frozen.

I quickly scan Princess Island. The Princesses have servants for everything – to care for their children, to rub their muscles, to teach them exercises, and to bring them food and drink. The Princesses wear very little clothing, but make up for it in covering themselves in sparkling, colorful gems. They all look the same and act the same, because they are the same. The princesses are an army of engineered duplicates of physical perfection, but are devoid of emotions like pride, self-sacrifice, and compassion. I don't belong here. I dart back into the ocean, kicking sand up as I run into the water. I jump in to my familiar surroundings and swim earnestly toward the Island of Power Queens.

By the time I reach the shore, I'm exhausted. My arms and legs burn and quiver as I stumble up on to the sand. The beach is deserted. Looking inland, I see shiny, tall buildings made of steel and glass. That must be where the Power Queens live. It's not far, so I walk toward the metallic towers. Once I arrive, everything seems cold and dark. Even though it's a tropical climate, the soaring structures nearly obliterate the sun and the sky. I listen intently, but I am unable to hear the singing of birds, the splashing of water, or the rustle of an ocean breeze. As I inspect the land, I find no flowers, no trees or any other signs of nature.

All I can hear is a clickety-clack sound. It's unfamiliar and foreign. I glance up and down the concrete pathways that line the space between the monstrous, polished structures. The tapping sounds grow louder and, for the first time, I spot a group of Power Queens.

As with the Princesses, I know they're female because we have the same parts. But again, I find that we are so dissimilar. Many of the Power Queens are lumpy, with broad behinds and large thighs. They all dress in a similar uniform, consisting of either dark pants or skirts, and topped off with plain shirts that are buttoned up the front. Their feet are wedged into some kind of tight contraption with stilts attached to the back. With every step, the stilts click against the hard ground. My feet, however, are barefoot and my steps are silent. Their skin is so pale that it's nearly translucent. Mine is dark and drenched by the sun. Their faces look like they are chiseled statues, forever carved into a worried scowl.

Most of the Power Queens seem to be held in a trance by some kind of rectangular device that they hold either to their ear or in front of them. Many of them talk directly into their rectangles, while others prod and push on them with their pointy fingers. They don't talk to one another. The Power Queens march up and down the concrete paths in hordes, yet they are each in isolation.

Humbly, I approach one of them, still nervous after things went so poorly with the Princess. "Excuse me, ma'am," I stutter, "could you help me?" She frowns at me with unabated disgust and revulsion. The Power Queen scrutinizes me as I stand in front of her dressed in my raggedy shorts and t-shirt, with my curly wild hair, and my tanned body. Then, she grunts in disapproval. "*You* want help?" she asks. "Yes, I do," I answer, "you see, I've been treading water in the ocean most of my life, not sure of where I fit in. It's time for me to find a home." Her look is intimidating as she says, "You want help? Get a job and help yourself." Then she stomps off.

Scorned, embarrassed, degraded, and in tears, I run back to the warm sandy shore and charge into the ocean. I relax as soon as the water caresses my body. A pod of dolphins encircles me and entertains me with flips and jumps. Below the surface of the water, their slick, rubbery skin gently rubs against my legs. They are trying to tell me what I should have known all along. I am home. Somewhere between the Island of Princesses and the Island of Power Queens, I belong. As much as I don't fit in on either of their islands, they don't belong in my sea. I realize the sun and moon have misled me and caused me to doubt myself. Never again will I allow myself to be led astray. I am content drifting in the water, somewhere between the two extremes.

. . .

Kate O'Reilley *is the author of two medical thrillers, and is well underway on writing her third novel. She is also a physician, who subsidizes her writing endeavors by practicing anesthesiology. Kate's goal is to eventually write full time and retire from medicine. She also writes a popular blog, katevsworld.com, where she demonstrates her satire and irreverent wit. In her spare time, Kate enjoys any ocean activity, running and spending time with her husband and daughter. Please visit Kate at kateoreilley.com or contact her by email @ kateoreilley@gmail.com.*

Fall's Fossils
by Diane Webster

Leaves blow across
the sidewalk imprinted
with one Fall's crop
like a trilobite fossil
hammered to light
from two slabs of rock
once millennium mud
hardened into museum stone
on display like this decade's
catch of ash leaves cemented.

Rain Thaw
by Diane Webster

Puddle collected
in low pavement
alive with starlings
splashing and stomping
feet and wings
in bathing frantic frolic
after last night's freezing
rain thawed.

Between the Lines
by Diane Webster

Soggy sheet of paper lies
on wet pavement
with tire treads squished
between the lines.
By afternoon, frayed
white scraps lift
a faltering wave
before disintegration.

. . .

Diane Webster's *challenge as a writer is to remain open to poetry ideas in everyday life and to write about those opportunities in an interesting manner. She enjoys writing letters and drives in the mountains. Diane's work has appeared in "Eunoia Review," "The Rainbow Rose," "The Hurricane Review" and other literary magazines.*